DUAL REALITIES

DUAL REALITIES
The Search for Meaning

Psychodynamic Therapy with Physically Ill People

Edited by
Ruth Archer

Foreword by
David M. Black

KARNAC

First published in 2006 by
Karnac Books
118 Finchley Road
London NW3 5HT

British Library Cataloguing in Publication Data

A C.I.P. for this book is available from the British Library

ISBN-13: 978-1-85575-415-7
ISBN-10: 1-85575-415-0

Edited, designed, and produced by Communication Crafts

Printed in Great Britain

www.karnacbooks.com

This book is dedicated to the memory of
Fay Cobb and Anne Neary
and to past, present, and future clients

CONTENTS

ACKNOWLEDGEMENTS   ix

ABOUT THE CONTRIBUTORS   xi

FOREWORD
       David M. Black   xv

Introduction
       Ruth Archer   1

1   Assessing clients with a serious physical illness
     or disability for psychodynamic therapy
       Gwen Evans   7

2   Emotional reactions to serious diagnosis
       Celia Nightall   18

3   Living with a life-threatening tumour:
     in search of meaning and creativity
       Dorothee Steffens   29

4   Avoiding the issues:
the consequences of poorly managed diabetes
Susan Berger   40

5   Living in the shadow of death
Lynda Snowdon   51

6   "A journey of a thousand miles begins with the first step"
Lavinia Chant and Rosemary Dixon-Nuttall   63

7   Working with dual realities: psychological and physical
Linette Hatfield   79

8   What did you say? What did you mean?
Michael Kelly   92

9   Becoming free
Anne Green   104

10   A life well lived: the challenge of progressive disability
Ruth Archer   112

11   Who am I, that I might become?
The spiritual dimension in work with people
who are seriously physically ill
Judy Parkinson   123

12   Inner worlds—outer realities.
The dying person in counselling and psychotherapy
Ruth Archer   136

13   Supervision of counsellors working with
seriously physically ill patients
Gertrud Mander   149

REFERENCES   159

INDEX   165

ACKNOWLEDGEMENTS

The Editor and authors of the individual chapters would like to acknowledge with gratitude the people who have given their permission for their session material to be published in this book.

We would also like to thank former colleagues from the Serious Physical Illness Counselling Service for their unfailing support during the preparation of this book. They are Valerie Knowles, Roswitha Keller, Erna Samuel, Maisie Murphy, Lorna Hill, Patti Wallace, and Anne Walsh.

We are indebted to a number of people for their advice and help with the book proposal and manuscripts, including Andrew Samuels, Helen Scoging, Pat Bolton, Judith Edwards, Gertrud Mander, and Celia Nightall. In addition, grateful thanks to Isobel Hathaway, Betty Raymond, and Mary Anne Coate, whose advice and technical expertise on the computer rescued the Editor on a number of occasions. Thanks also to Jean Roberts for reading the proofs.

Lastly, we wish to thank Val Potter and Lesley Murdin, Directors of WPF Counselling and Psychotherapy, for their support and encouragement, and David Black, Vice-Chair of WPF Trustees, for his ethical oversight and for writing the Foreword.

ABOUT THE CONTRIBUTORS

RUTH ARCHER originally trained in general nursing and midwifery. After working in Papua New Guinea for ten years, she returned to the United Kingdom and worked in the NHS before retraining as a psychoanalytic psychotherapist at the Westminster Pastoral Foundation, Kensington. She is registered with UKCP and was formerly Head of Counselling and Psychotherapy Services at the WPF. She is an Honorary member of the Foundation for Psychotherapy and Counselling, a Fellow of BACP, and a BACP-accredited supervisor. Ruth has published several articles in the nursing and counselling press, including a chapter on referral procedures in a BACP book, *NVQ/SVQ Level Three Counselling* (1999). She was also co-author of the research paper "The Effectiveness of a Voluntary Sector Psychodynamic Counselling Service" (*British Journal of Medical Psychology*, 73, Part 3, September 2000). She is now semi-retired and lives in Dorset.

SUSAN BERGER qualified as a counsellor with a diploma in Advanced Psychodynamic Counselling at WPF Counselling and Psychotherapy. Currently she works in private practice and in the NHS. She is a member of the Foundation for Psychotherapy and Counselling.

LAVINIA CHANT was born in London before the Second World War. As a child during that conflict she was evacuated for three years. After obtaining her school certificate she attended art school and then went on to receive her teaching credentials from Goldsmiths' College, London University. She taught art for London County Council schools for two and a half years. She left in the 1950s when she married an American and emigrated to Los Angeles, California, where she lived for almost thirty years. During that time she did volunteer work for the pre-school Headstart programme and also worked at the local primary school taking classes in art and remedial English and reading. She also designed and painted the sets for a High School drama production of three plays and illustrated the programme. Before leaving California Mrs Chant wrote a feature column for two Los Angeles newspapers. During her last years in California Mrs Chant also made presentations on a variety of topics to a local Fellowship society and helped write and illustrate their newsletter. She now lives in Greenwich, London.

ROSEMARY DIXON-NUTTALL trained as a sick-children's nurse before gaining further qualifications in general nursing, midwifery, and health visiting. After several posts in hospital and community nursing in England, she spent thirteen years in India, participating in the establishment of a community health project and subsequently teaching student nurses, before returning to England for retraining in counselling and psychotherapy. After obtaining a diploma in Psychodynamic Counselling, she undertook training in group psychotherapy at WPF. Later she qualified as an individual psychotherapist with the Association of Group and Individual Psychotherapy. She worked on the staff at WPF Counselling and Psychotherapy for twelve years and had a private practice in Sussex. She retired in July 2002.

GWEN EVANS trained as a psychodynamic counsellor and psychoanalytic psychotherapist at WPF Counselling and Psychotherapy. She works in clinical posts at WPF and has a private practice. She is a member of the Foundation for Psychotherapy and Counselling.

ANNE GREEN was born in 1946, suffering from cerebral palsy. She was one of a family of eight children. In order to obtain the treatment she needed, Anne spent her early childhood in an orthopaedic hospital, and later she attended a school for physically handicapped children. At the age of 17, she went to work in a centre for people disabled by cerebral palsy, where she made coat hangers and packed crayons in boxes. However, this work did not offer her sufficient stimulation, and she left when she was 20 to attend a college in Bristol, where she obtained five "O" levels and one "A" level. This opened the way to higher education, and after taking various courses, she is currently completing a degree through the Open University. Anne has contributed to the understanding of disablement issues by publishing three books and a number of articles in journals and magazines. Her next challenge is to complete a Master's Degree, and she plans to write her dissertation on "Independent Living for the Disabled".

LINETTE HATFIELD qualified as a counsellor with a Diploma in Advanced Psychodynamic Counselling at WPF Counselling and Psychotherapy. She completed her training with a year's placement in the Serious Physical Illness Counselling Service at WPF, and later she worked in the service as a staff counsellor for two years. She is a member of the Foundation for Psychotherapy and Counselling. She has a private practice and works for the mental health charity MIND, in Harrow.

MICHAEL KELLY qualified as a counsellor with a Diploma in Advanced Psychodynamic Counselling at WPF and the Roehampton Institute, University of Surrey, after which he completed an eighteen-month postgraduate placement in the Serious Physical Illness Counselling Service. He worked in the mental health sector of the NHS, offering counselling to people who attended a day-care centre. In 2000, he established the renal counselling service at Barts and the London NHS Trust. This service offers counselling to those diagnosed with end-stage renal disease and to their families. He contributed a chapter to a book entitled *Renal Care* and has presented papers at renal conferences at national and European level. He now lives in Ireland and is Counselling Coordinator for the Irish Kidney Association.

GERTRUD MANDER is an experienced psychoanalytic psychotherapist and supervisor. She is an Honorary member of the Foundation for Psychotherapy and Counselling, a Fellow of BACP, and a BACP-accredited supervisor. She was a staff member of WPF Counselling and Psychotherapy for twenty-five years, where she worked in the Training Department as a supervisor and organized the Training in Supervision. In the Counselling Service, she worked as a staff supervisor and supervised counsellors working in the Serious Physical Illness Counselling Service. She has published several papers on psychotherapy and supervision and has also published the book *A Psychodynamic Approach to Brief Therapy* (2000).

CELIA NIGHTALL qualified as a psychodynamic counsellor in 1984 and came into the counselling world with over twenty years' experience as a medical secretary in hospitals and in GP and private medical practice, and having been a Samaritan volunteer. She worked with the Serious Physical Illness Service at WPF Counselling and Psychotherapy as a clinical assessor and counsellor of mainly long-term clients for twelve years. Her experience also includes: private counselling practice; counselling coordination of a counselling service affiliated to WPF Counselling and Psychotherapy; research on the effect of counselling on suicide risk; and assisting in setting up a counselling service for people with cystic fibrosis. She has now retired from counselling.

JUDY PARKINSON trained as a general and a psychiatric nurse. She completed the Diploma in Advanced Psychodynamic Counselling and qualified in Individual Psychotherapy at WPF Counselling and Psychotherapy. She works part-time as a Clinical Nurse Specialist in Psychological Care at the Royal Marsden Hospital, Surrey. She is in private practice as a psychoanalytic psychotherapist.

LYNDA SNOWDON qualified as a teacher at Goldsmiths' College, University of London, and became head teacher of an infant school with a nursery unit. She was an author and consultant for Macmillan Education. As a volunteer she qualified and practised with MIND in their befriending service. She qualified as a counsellor with a Diploma in Advanced Psychodynamic Counselling at WPF and continued her training with a postgraduate placement specializing in clients with serious physical illnesses. She was appointed a member of staff at WPF and continued her counselling work within the specialist unit and in the general service until her retirement in 2001.

DOROTHEE STEFFENS is a Jungian analyst and a professional member of the Society of Analytical Psychology. She is a psychoanalytic psychotherapist (FPC/WPF) and works in private practice and as a training supervisor and psychotherapist for WPF Counselling and Psychotherapy.

FOREWORD

David M. Black

The Serious Physical Illness project of the WPF (WPF Counselling and Psychotherapy), one of the UK's largest organizations for counselling and counselling training, was set
up in 1984 to help patients suffering from serious, degenerative,
or terminal physical conditions. This was a pioneering venture,
strongly supported by Derek Blows, WPF's innovative Director at
the time. Ruth Archer in her Introduction outlines the history and
terms of reference of the project, and the chapters in this book are
all by members of its staff. I do not need to repeat what Archer
says, but I should add what she modestly omits: that she herself
was the inspirer and linchpin of the service from its inception. It
is safe to say that without Ruth Archer's conviction and commitment, this unique project could not have come into being.

To work with patients with severe physical disorders is unique-
ly challenging. Very often, though not always, what will have to
be faced is the closing-down of possibility, and sometimes the
final closure of death itself. Counsellors and psychotherapists are

David M. Black is a Member of the British Psychoanalytical Society and
Vice-Chair of WPF's Council of Management.

accustomed to having to work in the awareness that, however great their devotion, care, and skill, there can be no certainty that the outcome will be "improvement" or greater happiness for their patient. Nevertheless, in the ordinary course of counselling work, the lives of many patients do develop and find meaning, and counsellors may legitimately take great pleasure from that fact. Working with patients with deteriorating disability or severe illness confronts the counsellor with the sober reality of a situation that may offer no chance, or certainly no likelihood, of external improvement. Ruth Archer's own account (chapter 10) of working with a woman with a deteriorating condition caused by cerebral palsy gives us the feel of it. Archer speaks of having to cope with her own "rage" at the terrible limitations this gifted and courageous woman was increasingly forced to bear. We also hear (chapter 9) this patient's own account of her condition and her counselling. Judy Parkinson (chapter 11) describes working with an energetic young businessman, now approaching premature death from an AIDS-related illness. Parkinson worked hard with him until shortly before he died.

Work of this sort makes heavy emotional demands on the counsellor, in particular to recognize his or her own habitual defences against loss, diminishment, and recognition of the reality of death. Celia Nightall (chapter 2) gives a helpful overview of the range of "normal responses" of patients who have these conditions to face. Among them she includes "dread and awe" emotions, pointing to an ontological dimension where no one has the answers, and the counsellor is inevitably as vulnerable and lacking in knowledge as the patient. Gertrud Mander (chapter 13), who was supervisor to the Serious Physical Illness Service, speaks of "the constant temptation of omnipotent wishful thinking" to shut out the despair that can threaten both parties in these demanding encounters. In chapter 12 we hear of a woman with a terminal illness whose husband insisted on planning their next holiday abroad. When the counsellor finally put into words the reality that the woman was, in fact, going to die, she, the patient, declared her relief. "I felt I was going mad," she said. It is a salutary reminder that, in fact, manic defences—common and understandable as they may be in these situations—inflict madness and unreality on both ourselves and others.

Linette Hatfield (chapter 7) draws attention to a further innovative aspect of this work. This is that it involves a "dual focus". One focus is on the symbolic and transferential meanings of the patient's communication, as in all sound psychoanalytically based therapy. The other is the physical reality of the patient's body and its non-symbolic, factual fate. This duality necessarily involved departures, scrupulously discussed within the service, from the conventional formal boundaries of counselling sessions, to allow for home and hospital visits, arranged or accidental encounters with the patient's family and other carers, and such matters as whether or not to attend funerals. Issues of this sort turn up from time to time for every psychotherapist, but they had to be built in to the essential fabric of the thinking done by WPF's Serious Physical Illness team.

Overall, this book is a collection of moving and insightful contributions by dedicated clinicians, working in a very important specialized area. The great value of the work will, I think, be self-evident to readers, whether they are inside or outside the world of psychotherapy and counselling. Because of the cost of such counselling (increased by the need for home and hospital visits, and, by its nature, often done with patients with only very limited resources), the scale of the Serious Physical Illness Service had to be reduced following the difficult financial situation for charities at the close of the 1990s. As things improve, it is to be hoped that the service will once again be expanded and also that counsellors elsewhere may be inspired to take up this work. If so, this book provides admirable guidance to both the necessary precautions and the rewards of an extremely demanding, but extremely important, field for counselling activity. I commend it to you. (All royalties will go towards the costs of the WPF Serious Physical Illness Service.)

DUAL REALITIES

Introduction

Ruth Archer

The search for meaning exercises every human being at some level throughout life. At times of crisis or personal trauma, the need to make sense of what has happened becomes more urgent. Serious illness or an incurred disability is such a time. Illness may strike suddenly or have a gradual onset; either way, it stops us in our tracks and interrupts the normal progress of life. Whatever the outcome, it triggers the question: what does this mean?

* * *

The group of counsellors and psychotherapists working with ill people at WPF Counselling and Psychotherapy (formerly Westminster Pastoral Foundation) found that underlying all other issues that arose during the course of a life-threatening illness was a need for each person to discover its individual meaning for them. Many people who had already discovered meaning in their life prior to their illness had to rethink this in the light of their new experience of becoming seriously ill, which frequently changed their self-image—sometimes physically, but always emotionally.

As part of this process, a person will seek an explanation for his or her illness or condition. For it to be a random occurrence is often existentially stressful and makes coming to terms with the situation more difficult.

This book does not have all or perhaps any of the answers, but it records the experiences of some of the people who came for counselling between 1988 and 2001 at the WPF. All had a serious physical illness or disability, for which they sought psychotherapeutic help.

The Serious Physical Illness Counselling Service was first set up in the autumn of 1984 at the WPF premises in the Chelsea Methodist Church. Initially it was intended for people with cancer, but it soon became apparent that people with other illnesses were interested in using the service. Funding was received from the Greater London Council for two counsellors: these were Gill Russell, who did much of the early groundwork required to set up the service, and Fay Cobb. They were later joined by Ann Neary. These three, together with Marlene Heap, then Head of the WPF Counselling Service, whose idea it was to set up a specialist service, were supported by the Director, Revd Derek Blows. A conference was held for GPs and social workers in 1985, and there were consultations with local hospitals and with the national organizations Cancerlink and BACUP. As the numbers grew, other counsellors were recruited, including myself and several others who stayed to work in the service for many years, gaining considerable experience in this field of work.

Counsellors who expressed an interest were carefully selected. Some had nursing backgrounds, others came from a variety of different professions. All were qualified psychodynamic counsellors with some experience, who for one reason or another were keen to work in this particular field. It was necessary to be careful that counsellors were not unconsciously choosing this area of work to work something out for themselves. Anyone who was recently bereaved or who had a very ill relative or friend at the time of application was asked to wait and reapply after a mutually agreed period of time.

As the main WPF model is of once-weekly psychodynamic counselling, this is what was offered to clients.

* * *

After a while it became apparent that the premises at Chelsea were unsuitable, because of the number of stairs that clients had to climb. We also had no wheelchair access, so were unable to accommodate this group of people. We were very fortunate, therefore, when we were offered extra ground-floor accommodation at our Kensington site, in the William Kyle Centre (named after the Founder of WPF). This enabled us to provide wheelchair access and suitable toilet facilities. We moved there in April 1988, thanks to the assistance of our landladies, the Sisters of The Assumption.

From the beginning the designated counsellors did the assessments, and clients were allocated within the team. This meant that the waiting time was less and all concerned were aware of the caseload. Weekly supervision was provided, and this was increased in order to give maximum support to those working with very ill clients. A trained Family and Marital counsellor was added to the team, and this enabled us to see couples and families together, when the need arose. We were also fortunate to have our own receptionist to make appointments and answer the all-important first call made by a potential client. Sometimes a relative or main carer was seen rather than the ill person, as they were the most in need of help. We also held courses for other health care professionals and had telephone consultations with nurses and social workers.

One interesting aspect of the work was the difficulty we had in recruiting male staff to work in the service. In the thirteen years covered by this book, we had only two male counsellors, one of whom has contributed a chapter to the book. The reasons for this are not clear, as there was no shortage of interested female counsellors. During the 1990s we introduced a postgraduate programme, to enable newly qualified counsellors to gain experience. They spent eighteen months working and learning on the job and provided a valuable resource.

* * *

Probably the most innovative aspect of the work during the early years was the development of home visits. This innovation expanded the boundaries of psychodynamic work; it proved necessary mainly during long-term work, when the client became too ill to travel to the centre. Funding did not allow us to visit people at home from the beginning of their illness and was only agreed after very careful consideration. Guidelines were drawn up for counsellors making home or hospital visits, and these were only made at the client's request. It did mean, however, that the work was not interrupted by the client's physical incapacity, provided that he or she wished to continue. In the case of a terminal illness, the counselling continued as long as was appropriate for all concerned. Inevitably, in the latter situation the counsellor met with other family members, and then boundaries had to be skilfully negotiated.

* * *

Over the years, clients presented with a wide range of illnesses and physical conditions including cancer, AIDS, multiple sclerosis, ME, blood disorders, and some rather rare conditions, including those of genetic origin. In addition, we saw people with a wide range of congenital or acquired disabilities, including cerebral palsy, visual and hearing impairments, and paraplegia, the latter often but not always the result of an accidental injury. Later we saw people following lung, heart, or liver transplants. We also set up a special project within the service for young people with cystic fibrosis, called Breathing Space, in conjunction with the Cystic Fibrosis Trust. On occasion, because we were a flexible service, we also offered short-term work to young people with learning difficulties, whose problem often contained a physical component such as epilepsy.

In 1992, we set up a therapy group for clients who expressed an interest in groupwork. One of our team, Rosemary Dixon-Nuttall, who was a qualified group psychotherapist, ran the group for six to eight clients, on an open-ended basis, until 2001. During that time the group included people with a variety of physical problems, as well as some who joined the group who were physically well. This arrangement seemed to work well, especially as the group members came from different cultural and ethnic backgrounds.

Counsellors working in the service were not, of course, immune from the illnesses that afflict the rest of humanity. Counsellors did become ill, sometimes seriously. Such instances provided the opportunity to understand more from the patient's viewpoint, as well as discovering the counsellor's own source of meaning.

It was important for the staff to keep up to date, and meetings were held at least three times a year. These usually focused on a specific topic, sometimes with an invited speaker, in order that we could look in depth at areas of particular difficulty or interest, such as ME or AIDS. On the team, both counsellors and psychotherapists functioned equally. Little differentiation was made when clients were allocated, except to ensure as far as possible a good-enough match, depending on the team members' level of experience and expertise.

In 1989, a colleague did a piece of research, using client–counsellor couples, on emotional adaptation to serious illness (Wallace, 1989). From this we learnt of the high level of suicidal ideation, of which the counsellors were largely unaware, among the clients interviewed. This insight was to inform our work for many years to come.

* * *

The authors contributing to this book have worked in the service for varying periods of time. They formed a multicultural team, who brought insights from many different backgrounds. Three of the contributors are service users, and we are grateful for their special contribution in the form of both chapters and illustrations. We are indebted to the people whose therapeutic experiences feature in the chapters that contain case material. There have generously given us their permission to use material from their sessions, without which this book would not have been written.

* * *

Experience, thought, and technique are the cornerstones of the therapeutic process. The book reflects this. Comprising thirteen chapters, the book begins and ends with the technical framework for the work, the assessment of physically ill or disabled people for psychotherapy, and the supervision of therapists working with those individuals. Six chapters are predominantly concerned with case material, and these are interspersed with chapters that focus more on process and technique. The words patient/client and counsellor/therapist are used interchangeably.

* * *

During their working life most therapists will meet patients/ clients who are disabled or who develop a life-threatening illness. Therapist are often unprepared for this encounter, which raises questions about their own mortality and the meaning of life and death. This book aims to show how therapists can work effectively with ill or disabled people, by facing their fears, by adjusting their technique, and, above all, by learning from the patient while accompanying them on their journey.

CHAPTER ONE

Assessing clients with a serious physical illness or disability for psychodynamic therapy

Gwen Evans

Psychodynamic therapy is based on psychoanalytic theory and practice. The central principle is that distress has been caused by events and modes of relating in early life of which we are no longer aware. From the earliest years of the practice of this model of therapy, its application has extended. One facet of this extension is working with people who have a serious illness or disability. Impairment of bodily function can happen at any time from uterine life on and may be temporary or permanent. Sometimes impairment is stable or can change. These states of being will have resonances with a patient's internal world and past life experiences, though this will not be readily apparent to them. There can be little dispute that in Western culture the dominant model of disease is biologically based, which means that a patient's emotional responses to it can sometimes be ignored or given only scant attention. Conversely, any attempt to apply psychological understanding alone "undermines the reality of the disease" (Sontag, 1983, p. 59). The notion of physical versus psychological does not give due regard to the lively forces at work in body and mind which impact and are interdependent the one with the other. It is the interrelating of body and mind that gives credibility to the need for psychological therapies to be made available to patients with a serious physical illness or disability, many of whom are distressed. I wish to briefly describe a developmental paradigm from which the effects of impaired bodily function on the mind can be understood.

Winnicott (1949) describes how in healthy early development, psyche and soma are indistinguishable:

> Here is a body and the psyche and the soma are not to be distinguished except according to the direction from which one is looking. One can look at the developing body or at the developing psyche. I suppose the word psyche here means the *imaginative elaboration of somatic parts, feelings, and functions* that is, of physical aliveness. [p. 244]

He goes on:

> Gradually the psyche and the soma aspects of the growing person become involved in a process of mutual interrelation. [p. 244]

It is the "interrelating between psyche and soma" which for healthy development requires "a continuity of being" (Winnicott). This emerges out of the early mother–infant relationship, when a mother provides a psychological and physiological protection for her baby. Such a provision is made possible through a mother's intense identification with her baby. Sue Gerhardt (2004) writes: "Babies need a care-giver who identifies with them so strongly that the baby's needs feel like hers; he is still physiologically and psychologically an extension of her" (p. 23). The routines involved in early infant care around feeding, nappy changing, bathing, and soothing a distressed state need to be experienced by the baby as rhythmic and under his omnipotent control. It is the mother's ability to respond appropriately to her infant that facilitates development. For body–mind integration, the need for continuity in infancy is absolute and the cornerstone on which mental health is founded. A mother's gradual introduction of some failure to this continuity is a further important developmental stage. The process of allowing her baby to separate is vital and marks the beginning of disillusionment for the baby. By the end of this stage, the mother "will be perceived as separate and available for a genuine as opposed to an omnipotent relationship" (Fonagy, 2001, p. 95). The positive determinants for a successful outcome at this stage are numerous. A healthy mother will be able to slowly withdraw from a state of psychological merger with her baby while continuing to be devoted to his care. A less good outcome has profound implications for the aetiology of psychosomatic illness and hypochondriacal states. In this way a developmental perspective provides a framework from which understanding can be given as to the effect on the psyche of somatic disturbance.

Illness and disability disrupt and compromise a "continuity of being" that resonates with experiences when at a stage of total dependence. When a diagnosis of disability or serious physical illness is made, alongside good medical management, the care a patient receives should include emotional support that gives recognition to the disruption. For some, this will be adequate, whereas for others a more structured framework will be helpful, even necessary, and a contract for psychodynamic therapy may be appropriate. This model of therapy offers a space for exploration from which meaning can emerge. However, it is not beneficial to all, and one task of the initial interview is for an assessment to be made as to whether a patient can take up and use this mode of counselling. Another style of therapy may be more appropriate or a recommendation made to a specialist service. For example, a wheelchair user who wants advice about ramps but is not motivated to access her or his internal world will be unable to make use of psychodynamic counselling.

* * *

At WPF Counselling and Psychotherapy, the setting for the assessment interview and most ongoing counselling for this client group is a building with ground-floor rooms, wheelchair access, and adapted facilities. The building is set within grounds in a beautiful garden. The institutional backcloth sets up a dynamic, as does the fact that the patient and assessment counsellor are unlikely to meet again. If the outcome of the interview is a recommendation for psychodynamic counselling, it is usual practice for the patient to be allocated another counsellor for ongoing therapy. There is also the wider setting, which includes the social, cultural, political, and religious contexts. A narrower yet crucial aspect is the way the interview is set up and managed. This results from a view of what the encounter between patient and counsellor is about. However, it is the internal framework within the counsellor, and that which it is possible to establish with a patient, that provides the most important setting.

Approaches to assessment interviews differ widely. At WPF the usual procedure is for one interview of approximately 90 minutes' duration to be offered, with the expectation that following this a recommendation can be made. This will include gaining some understanding of the referral. When it has not been possible for an assessor to arrive at a recommendation, a further interview is offered with another assessment counsellor or consultant psychiatrist. The task is of such remarkable complexity that I do not know of any colleague who regards the confined time frame of one interview as adequate. However, limited resources make it a necessity and put constraints on what is offered. The challenge of the less than ideal is about the attempt to undertake a demanding job well enough in the circumstances.

Within the psychodynamic model, there exist various theoretical frameworks in relation to assessment. Each has a different emphasis. On the one hand there "is the idea that there is no difference between the analytic process in the first meeting and that in any other analytic meeting" (Ogden, 1989, p. 170). Clearly the stance of not regarding the initial interview as a complete piece of work in itself is very different from the aim of assessment being "to obtain sufficient evidence to enable him to prescribe an appropriate intervention" (Malan, 1979, p. 210). The more purist analytic attitude has its place (with an emphasis on creating, not taking, a history), though a counter-viewpoint is that "interviewers should not behave like a caricature of an analyst" (Coltart, 1987). Coltart places strong emphasis on an assessment interview being one in which the assessor has to work in a more active way than is usually the case during ongoing counselling. She argues for the "need to establish a certain rapport and keep it going . . . to find out about this stranger's inner world. This may involve some questioning, some interpretation, some link making comments, sympathy expressed only in your whole attitude of extremely attentive listening and some concise summarising of your own views towards the end of the interview" (pp. 133–134).

The style of assessment Coltart advocates is readily applicable to the group of patients I am addressing. It is important to ascertain a medical history, especially as it relates to what the patient presents as "the problem": the disability or illness. It may be that the disability or illness is not the problem a patient presents for counselling with, or is not the most important aspect of his or her life. However, it would be important to note what does not get spoken about and to consider its meaning. It could be that a patient with a disability holds a fundamental belief that he or she cannot be understood by an able-bodied counsellor. If the disability or illness is a disowned or hated part of him/herself, then the counsellor might be expected to hate or not recognize it too. For some, there will be no escape from being needy, physically and emotionally. An assessment of how the patient tolerates his or her dependency needs will go some way to informing how any therapeutic alliance might be taken up. There is a lot going on in society about eradicating disability, which has resulted in people fighting to be visible and heard. To defend against not being wanted and hated, people may become politicized while internalizing the pain and rage. All of this will have an impact on the assessment counsellor, the process of assessment, and the ongoing work. Noting whether a disability is congenital or the result of a degenerative process or accident, and enquiring when symptoms were first noted and at what stage an illness became serious, provides a baseline record. This should include information about current treatment regimens, including medication. Also requested is the patient's signed consent for contact to be made with his or her GP or medical consultant, who will be informed of the patient having made contact with the WPF and asked if there might be any contraindications for psychodynamic work to be embarked upon (at WPF this is the practice only when there is a significant medical history). It is obvious that this is all weighted towards a biomedical model and is time consuming, and the patient will have been through a similar process with medical staff, possibly on numerous occasions. However, it is negligent not to acquire this information which gives due regard to "the reality of the disease".

While this mode of assessment interview is not "creating a history" (Ogden, 1989, p. 191), it is possible to maintain a modified psychoanalytic stance that is qualitatively different from a medical one and a patient will experience it as such. Another baseline reading needs to be formulated, which may be more tentative and relates to the patient's internal world. One theoretical framework for this is that of object relations. With regard to assessment interviews, the clinical application of this is in three areas: the "current life situation, infantile object relationships, and the transference relationship" (Hinshelwood, 1991). Hinshelwood summarizes that "from these core object relationships a point of maximum pain can be hypothesised" (pp. 166–167). A function of this is to make a psychodynamic formulation that, alongside other factors, informs the recommendation made as an outcome of the interview. (Some clarification is perhaps necessary, in that "a point of maximum pain" refers here to psychological pain.) A major aspect of the patient's "current life situation" will be serious illness or disability, and usually the interview will start with this or with something relating to it. While obtaining a history, the analytic stance referred to above is one of actively listening to how this is given and noting the impact it is having on oneself, on the patient's life, and on those around him or her. The nature of relationships with external objects (family members, colleagues, medical staff) spoken about will give some indication of an internal-object relationship through which it is possible to discern those of early infancy. The third area Hinshelwood highlights is that of the transference relationship, which is the one the patient has with the assessor. This is largely spontaneously produced, determined by childhood, and starts in phantasy way before the interview takes place.

* * *

A black woman presented for an assessment interview having had a stroke a year previously as a complication of a serious blood disorder. This has resulted in one side of her body feeling heavy and weak. While accompanying her from the waiting area, I noted a marked impairment of her ability to walk, though she did so unaided. At the outset she seemed cautious. She described physical restraints impeding progress and spoke of fears about becoming paralysed. As her history unfolded, it became clear that emotional restraint during her childhood had produced massively bottled-up resentment. Her father's love was totally conditional. He was her hero, for whom she never felt good or pretty enough. Her younger brother was her mother's preferred child. At a young age she was sent to live in her parents' country of origin for three years with relatives who hit her. She felt banished from her home in England and unlovable. She stated she has no relationships as she repeatedly pushes people away and, subsequent to her worsening physical health, had lost her employment.

From this brief vignette the current life situation of the client is one of physical illness and partial disability affecting her continuity of being. The infantile relationships are fickle and rejecting. In the transference, initial caution shifted to idealization. I understood this to be a defensive manoeuvre to avoid the pain of her depression, which she was struggling to hold at bay. A tentative hypothesis with regard to the point of maximum pain is the inevitability of rejection.

* * *

One of the other factors especially pertinent to this client group is for consideration to be given as to the extent that physical pain or medication might be affecting the patient's psychological state. Pain, serious illness, and disability give rise to heightened levels of stress and depleted levels of energy. A supportive psychodynamic stance may be helpful in its provision of an auxiliary ego function which is containing. Often some psychodynamic understanding can be added over time. Suitability for psychodynamic counselling should include some assessment of the degree of ego strength the patient has with which to tolerate what the work entails.

Mr M

Mr M was referred to the WPF by a psychologist at his local hospital. He had been attending weekly sessions with her for a period of about five months, and this contract had ended. My first impression on meeting with Mr M was to note his smart business suit, slightly tinted glasses, and mature demeanour. A white man in his early thirties, he appeared wearisome and serious. He presented feeling depressed and sometimes suicidal. Diagnosed with diabetes when a child, he was experiencing deteriorating physical health and anticipating kidney and pancreas transplants. Mr M started by telling me that his sessions with the psychologist had been helpful with regard to his level of depression, which had lifted, whereas his non-compliance about blood testing to manage his diabetic state continued. It became clear that while Mr M had a good knowledge of his condition and an intellectual understanding about the necessity for monitoring his glucose levels for insulin regulation, he neglected to manage this appropriately. The complications that had developed secondary to his diabetes were, in part, due to his inability to consistently comply with the measures necessary to control it. While his actions are puzzling, the outcome was shocking. Mr M spoke of having retinopathy (an eye complication of diabetes). At the age of 21, he lost his sight on and off for a year. Subsequent treatment was helpful, but impaired function led to his becoming registered partially sighted. He described symptoms of neuropathy and renal damage. For him to stay alive is a struggle. He "partly feels he should not be here", and suicidal ideation revolved around overdosing on insulin (a course of action readily available).

The emphasis during the early part of the interview on his deteriorating physical condition gave due regard to this reality. Perhaps he was more interested or preoccupied with the physical, or anticipated that I might be. It is possible this has been the case all of his life. Many medical consultations over years would have appropriately addressed the physical reality, which was clearly becoming ever more tragic. However, another reality began to emerge as I explored further.

Born in East Africa, where his parents worked as expatriate teachers, he is third in a sibship of four. The family moved to another African country when he was aged 3 years, and it was there that he was diagnosed as diabetic, at the age of 6. Shortly after this he was molested by a male friend of his parents. A further move took place when aged 8, and at the age of 10 he became a boarder at a school in England. During the first few years there he felt depressed and longed to return to Africa. Mr M spoke of stealing money from staff and, on one occasion, was seen by a psychiatrist. By the time his parents finally agreed that he could return to

Africa, he had decided to stay and study for "O" and "A" levels. Mr M read law at university, where he started with high ideals, ideas of justice, and altruistic notions about serving the underdog. Disillusionment quickly set in, and he finally left law when taking Articles because of deteriorating eyesight. His subsequent employment history has been in the charity sector, where he held influential positions. However, he frequently changes jobs, and at interview was experiencing his female boss as an incompetent bully.

Throughout his discourse Mr M spoke with clarity. He appeared to hold little by way of any expectations of me, and though he responded positively to my interest I sensed he felt unworthy of it. I noted themes of disruption, physical illness, abuse, separation, and a regard for fair action towards others. As I wondered about a lack of protection and level of deprivation, I made comment on how his family appeared as shadowy figures in his narrative.

Until this point in the interview my countertransference had felt rather deadened and sad. Suddenly this became very alert as Mr M spoke of the "high-level tension" between his parents. Linking this information with my thoughts about a lack of protection and deprivation, I explored how Mr M had felt in the face of parental conflict. He spoke of neglect which took the form of little attention being given to his diagnosis of diabetes. Instead of providing their young son with appropriate support, he experienced his parents as defensive to the extent that diabetes could barely be discussed. His father could not tolerate illness, and his mother felt guilty. The kind of neglect that results from having parents preoccupied with their own emotional needs can be very frightening. Here was evidence of a "continuity of being" being affected on a number of different levels. Pancreatic function could no longer produce the necessary levels of insulin to stabilize his blood glucose. His condition contributed to further tensions between his parents. Management of his diabetes involved four insulin injections a day. Initially this was regulated by urine testing, but from his mid-teens "home glucose testing" has been available. Mr M is unable to sustain doing this beyond two to three weeks at a stretch, which means his diabetes is poorly controlled. He understood this to be a denial of his condition. My thoughts were to wonder about his actions as a form of control and an act of revenge on his parents. It could be that failing to comply acts as a container for his rage and holds him together at a psychic level. The need to take care of himself perhaps contributes to an intensity of feelings of loneliness. Mr M acknowledged feeling lonely but stated that it is his preference to be alone. While this comment may demonstrate a tolerance of this state, it is possibly indicative of struggles with dependency. From this viewpoint the regular routine of insulin injections four times a day might provide a consoling reliability in the absence of a comforting other. The physical invasions of needle into subcutaneous tissue is putting something into himself that keeps him alive. Yet his repeated inability to establish a consistency of monitoring blood glucose levels has produced serious self-damage. Joseph (1989) writes that patients who compulsively repeat are dealing with potentially overpowering unconscious anxieties relating "primarily to problems stimulated by dependence on the primary object". In an attempt to master the anxieties, there is a link "with the achievement of a particular balance between destructiveness and love, and how the very nature of this balance in itself can lead to no progress, but only to a blind compulsion to repeat" (p. 17).

Mr M has been unable to investigate what is going on inside himself with regard to this compulsion. He has a clear awareness of a passive repetition of events over which he experiences having no control. Unconsciously this repeats the trauma of the abuse. What he cannot think about and process gets enacted. Self-harm is a means of attack that provides an outlet for aggressive impulses. This becomes destructive when feelings are not adequately contained and originates in not having a reliable continuity of experience from primary care-givers. It appears that the internalization of a stabilizing protective object with whom he could safely be vulnerable is too fragile. My hypothesis was to view this as the point of maximum pain. I made an interpretation that took into account this vulnerability as experienced in the transference and made a link with his current life context and infantile relationships. This provided Mr M with a means of understanding his struggle in terms of the dynamics involved, and he appeared to find this helpful. Psychodynamic counselling offers a chance to work through this struggle. At one level, he demonstrated enough readiness to look at this in greater depth. However, I wondered how much his physiological and psychological vulnerabilities would enable him to tolerate the process.

Mr M has a serious illness, and his condition is deteriorating. There was evidence of good-enough physiological function for him to be on a waiting list for organ transplants. During the assessment interview, Mr M demonstrated holding some hope, which needs sustaining. My recommendation for Mr M to be offered a contract for psychodynamic counselling placed emphasis on a choice for life, and the tentative hope he holds for change.

CHAPTER TWO

Emotional reactions to serious diagnosis

Celia Nightall

S uch is the impact of a serious illness on a person's life, it is unlikely ever to be forgotten. The life that person was used to changes and may never be the same again. Later, after recovery, or when he or she has come to terms with the situation, the day he or she was given the diagnosis will always be remembered—as will the effect it had on his or her life and family.

I counselled people who had to cope with physical illness and/or disabilities for many years, and so I have been able to observe their emotional reactions. This chapter is based on these observations, on experience I gained working in hospitals prior to becoming a counsellor, and on a more personal experience of illness. Insights have also been gained from relevant conferences and material written by professionals working in the field. The reactions described extend beyond those experienced at the actual time of the diagnosis to those experienced as the effects of the illness and/or disability become apparent. The aim of the chapter is to help counsellors understand the range of these normal responses; however, as each client's experience will be different, I have not included how an individual therapist might work with this material in counselling sessions.

Various emotional reactions are experienced, which may happen in almost any order, overlap, occur concurrently, or be arrested for various reasons, all according to a person's individual pathology, his or her personal history or life script or experience of others suffering from the same or a similar problem, and what he or she has learnt from books, television programmes, the Internet, or articles in newspapers. The reactions will also be affected by what the doctor has or has not said, his attitude and the manner in which he told that particular person his or her diagnosis.* They are also dependent on what the diagnosis actually is and what the person knows about the condition.

Initial or early reactions

When a person has started to develop symptoms of an illness, she has the difficulty of living in *a state of not knowing* what is causing the physical symptoms, which means she is living in a sort of no-man's-land, not being able to feel or consider herself as well and normal because of the symptoms but not being officially ill because of the lack of diagnosis. This can make her continually anxious about what she thinks might or might not be wrong with her, causing her to search medical books or the Internet or to seek other medical opinions. Without a concrete diagnosis, it is more difficult for the patient or client to get an internal picture of where she is or where she is going, and that can cause much anxiety.

If someone has been suffering various symptoms for some time, wondering what is going on with her body, the diagnosis can be a *relief*. This could be because she has been fantasizing that there is something even worse wrong, or worse in her eyes, or because she has felt that her symptoms seem bizarre or puzzling, making it difficult for her to pluck up courage to consult her primary-care doctor. Sufferers of multiple sclerosis may have such feelings before a diagnosis is finally made, and they sometimes have their symptoms misunderstood and attributed to stress or their imagination, even though they feel sure there is something really wrong

---

*I shall refer to doctors as male and the patients or clients as female, for the sake of clarity.

with them. Neurological symptoms can seem very strange when first experienced by a person with no knowledge of physiology or neurological illness. A person may have been seeking many medical opinions to find out what is wrong in the case of some of the more obscure diseases, so that to receive a diagnosis finally is a great relief. It may also be a relief because she may have had an idea of what is probably wrong, but her doctor has not actually told her the diagnosis, perhaps because he thinks she could not cope with it, or because he thinks he has told her but her anxiety has prevented her from hearing what was said, particularly if technical language has been used. Another reason for this is that the doctor, too, has suspected what the diagnosis might be but has been unable to give it until totally certain, either through investigation or until there is a combination of various symptoms and objective clinical signs. The patient or client may have gone through tremendous anxiety while searching for or awaiting the diagnosis, which brings to an end the uncertainty.

Shock may absolutely "freeze" a person. The shock at first hearing the diagnosis may cause her to hyperventilate, making her feel dizzy and sick, she may actually faint or have other physical symptoms, such as feeling cold and shivery. She may have a dry mouth, tightness in her chest, weak legs. Mentally she may feel stunned, struck dumb, so that she literally cannot speak. She may cry inconsolably, may react with anger, and scream out in distress. The world around her may not feel real; she may not feel real. What is going on around her may seem to recede, as if she is not part of it. She may feel she is in a dream, a bad one. In bad shock, a person will not be able to participate in everyday activities as before. She may cease to take proper care of herself for a time. She may not hear what is said to her, or she may hear it but it is just words without meaning. She may become full of despair. When the initial shock has worn off, other feelings will come along, the order of which will vary according to a person's personal psychology. It is possible also that a person will defend against experiencing these feelings, which may become somatized, thus producing additional physical symptoms. She may lose her appetite, be unable to sleep at night, or, as an escape from emotional pain, comfort-eat or feel exhausted and want to sleep all the time. (These physical symptoms can accompany other emotional reactions.)

Disbelief is an emotional reaction that may happen immediately on hearing the diagnosis, or later as a form of denial. The type of comment a patient may make is, "I feel all right. The doctor must have made a mistake!" Or, "I can't believe I'm so ill when I feel all right—the lump taken out didn't even hurt. The doctors must be wrong!" Disbelief may occur especially when a serious illness has been picked up accidentally, as it were, when a person is having a routine check-up, perhaps for insurance purposes, or has undergone a routine well-woman screening, for example.

Denial may happen because the patient is not ready to take in the diagnosis, not ready to hear it yet, perhaps realizing unconsciously that her emotional conditions are not strong enough yet because of her personal psychology or because of current life conditions. It may occur because of tremendous conscious or unconscious fears for herself and her family. Denying she is ill, she may not take appropriate care of herself, thus exacerbating her symptoms. For instance, a person with multiple sclerosis in denying her condition may not make allowances for the fatigue, thus getting incredibly exhausted. A diabetic may not take care to balance her intake of carbohydrate and her dosage of insulin, not do her daily blood sugar, the result of which can be very dangerous. A person in denying her condition may decide not to take the prescribed medication, thus putting great strain on her heart if she has a heart condition, for example.

There are feelings of *despair, grief, and sadness.* A feeling of upset and tears may occur at the time of being given a diagnosis, soon after, or soon after the initial shock has worn off. It may initially have been triggered by fear and the serious countenance of the patient's relatives or loved ones or the doctor concerned. The stage of real deep grief will probably take longer to reach; it may be one of the final stages to be gone through before reaching a stage of good-enough acceptance. After the patient or client has accepted her diagnosis, she may continue to go through short grieving phases, as, indeed, one can do for almost ever after the death of a loved one. An illness, chronic or progressive, fractures a person's personal autobiography—the dreams or plans she had for the future have to be worked on, changed. She has to grieve for her lost future and for the healthy person she once was, which in effect has now gone. All this takes time. If a discomforting symptom is cured, a symptom the patient may have got used to so that it has become part of her, then she may find she needs to grieve for that also.

The tendency to *self-pity*, present in us all, is likely to surface as part of the patient's response to her illness. This may occur soon after she has received her diagnosis or if she feels that the sympathy and attention she deserves is not forthcoming. However, if it continues for too long, it may impede her progress and will need to be explored.

Feelings caused by *personal reactions to authority figures* such as doctors and other medical staff will arise according to the individual's personal life script. They may make her hospital treatment, for instance, more traumatic than it might otherwise be, perhaps because her doctor reminds her of a disliked or forbidding family member, making it difficult for her to relate to him. It may make it difficult for her to ask the questions she would really like to ask, and so on. It may make her frightened of hospital visits.

Predominant emotions associated with illness

Regret and guilt may be part of the grieving process, may be part of the anger process. The sort of thoughts going though the patient's mind will be rather like this: "I wish I had done so and so when I had the chance—now it's too late." Or, "I should have done so and so and then I wouldn't have got ill." It may be that the illness or disability is experienced as a punishment.

Thoughts of *recrimination and resentment* may occur at any stage. A patient or client may look back at her life and wonder if her lifestyle or certain past actions have contributed to or caused her illness, or she may feel that it is a punishment for past actions. She may wonder if her doctors have carried out the appropriate investigations, at an early enough stage or if they have given her the appropriate treatment. Taking this further, she may resent her medical or surgical treatment, considering it has made her feel worse. There may be more intense paranoid feelings triggered by invasive treatment.

Anxiety may be caused by the suppression of such feelings as anger and fear. It will be caused by worry about how the patient is going to cope physically and financially, about how loved ones may react to her illness or disability, be about the course of her illness and possible or probable future symptoms and their effect on her life. Anxiety can cause physical symptoms like the ones mentioned as a possible reaction to shock—insomnia, loss of appetite, or increased hunger—or may cause a client to resort to the comfort of alcohol.

A patient or client may be afraid of how their loved ones will react to her diagnosis, may be afraid a partner or spouse will not stick by her—so much so she may possibly keep her illness, or at least the diagnosis, secret. There will be fear of the unknown, of dying, of leaving behind loved ones, of pain, of paralysis. There may be fear of the treatment—chemotherapy, radiotherapy, further surgery—or of the development of further symptoms, of being bed-bound, of having to be permanently in a wheelchair, for example.

Depression can become very severe. It occurs because of repressed anger, because of fear of what is happening to the person, because of general dispiritment, often with good reason. It may well be an emotional reaction occurring soon after receiving the diagnosis because of repression of other feelings, or because of other feelings being unacceptable.

A person with a life-threatening illness, or with a chronic disability or disabling illness, may well feel life is not worth living any more, that life in this state, as it now is, is not worth living. She may feel that life is not worth living in this pain, in this exhaustion, or that the quality of her life is not worth staying alive for. It may be that the depth of her depression, due to repressed anger, makes her want to take the anger out on herself, kill off the ill part of herself. In my experience, the majority of my clients had felt or felt *suicidal*, and it is important that the counsellor brings the subject into sessions as soon as it feels right to do so.

Anger is healthy and is the most powerful of all the feelings and one that might be suppressed. There should be anger that the illness, disease, or disability has happened to the patient. There should be anger at what it has done to her life, her spouse's life, her children's lives. There may be anger at her hospital treatment, or lack of it. There may well be recrimination, as already mentioned, and bitterness. There may be anger at the way she has been treated by doctors or family for a multitude of reasons. There may be danger that her future plans now have to be changed. Anger and frustration may be triggered when she finds she cannot now do something she used to be able to do. The most difficult aspect of anger when it is caused by the development of an illness or disability is that rarely is there a person or object of some kind to be angry at, and this makes it difficult to express the anger. This difficulty is often a reason given by clients for being unable to do so, albeit this reason is also a defence against expressing anger. The anger for what has happened has to be expressed, even, as it were, into thin air, and the energy that goes with the anger has to be expressed in some way that feels right for each particular client. I have found that some clients use up this energy by hard work—polishing or floor scrubbing, for example. Sometimes it is just necessary to feel that energy coming out, and somehow visualize it doing so. Often clients displace their anger and its energy, and they need help to express it appropriately. Anger can prevent recognition of real pleasures and abilities that could continue to be enjoyed.

The struggle for acceptance and meaning

There may be *withdrawal* and a sense of *isolation and loneliness*. Because of becoming absorbed by so many other feelings, or because the person may perhaps feel she has failed somehow because of her illness, has perhaps let others down, or let herself down in some way (or, indeed, projects these feelings and feels that others have let her down), she may withdraw. It will seem to others that she has withdrawn. Friends and family may experience this as a punishment, as if she has decided not to give them attention or acknowledgement because they have let her down in some way. They may feel guilty and impotent—and perhaps she has unconscious reasons for wanting them to feel so. A patient may withdraw because of the reaction to her illness by her friends and family: if those around her cannot cope, they may react in a way that denies the patient her illness and may make light of it unrealistically. Feelings arising out of her diagnosis can cover up her previous real feelings to her loved ones, so that it seems to the relatives that she doesn't love them any more or her desire and ability to love and care for others may be lost, hopefully temporarily. She may think that others cannot understand how she feels because they are not going through what she is going through, not suffering her illness, and this will make her feel isolated. In truth, only she is suffering what she is suffering—a lonely experience!

Suffering physical illness or disability may make a person feel *out of control* of her life because she may have to alter aspects of how she lives: she may be in and out of hospital, having to be looked after; she may have to use appliances to help with the activities of daily living; she may be in a wheelchair. This sense may be exacerbated by the way she is treated by those close to her or by hospital care, which can be both infantilizing and institutionalizing, causing regression.

Connecting with this can be a sense of *loss of personal identity* because she now feels she is an ill person rather than a well person, which in turn causes feelings of *depletion*. Because of the physical effects of a disease, patients may feel depleted: they cannot keep up with other people for various reasons, cannot carry out the same activities perhaps just through fatigue or through the effects of chemotherapy, radiotherapy, or surgery. They may be unable to work or may have to work part-time. Their image of themselves is changed. They may have to live on a lower income, perhaps benefits, and so have to change their spending habits, shop differently, go out less or not be able to go out at all with friends or family. A woman may feel less attractive as a woman, or know she actually does look less attractive. If she is disabled in some way, unable to move as fluidly as she once did, this may make a woman feel less good, as she feels ungraceful, less feminine. A man may feel he has lost his athletic prowess. He may lose the bulk of his muscles, making him feel weedy and weak. Certain diseases mean certain operations have to be carried out. For example, cancer of the breast may mean a mastectomy, with all this entails, a feeling of loss of femininity, not being totally a woman any more. Likewise, a hysterectomy will bring about this feeling, the womb like the breasts being symbols of femininity. If the disease necessitates the removal of part of the body, then there needs to be grieving for what the patient has lost. If a man has to have an operation like an orchidectomy, then he may be worried about his future sexual performance and potency.

Sometimes, when a person loses something, she is able to replace it with something else; however, when she realizes her life may change irrevocably as she is losing or may lose an essential part of her being—her health—which helps to define who she is and so gives her life meaning, this can be extremely hard to accept. She may feel or fear part of her is being or will be annihilated, so that she will never be the same again and she cannot survive, or does not want to do so in the state she imagines she will be in. Therefore *suicidal feelings* may well emerge and should always be taken seriously by the counsellor.

Feelings of *distaste and horror* may be caused because of drastic surgery, by such operations as mastectomy or operations that cause a sudden change in body shape so that the body the client knew and was familiar to her becomes strange, unfamiliar, does not look like her. Sometimes people develop keloid scars that can look unsightly and cause distress. If an individual's appearance has been of great importance before, and if he or she is a self-conscious person, much distress, horror, and distaste may be experienced. These feelings may cause depression or anger, and a lot of work has to be done to help that person come to terms with how he or she now is.

Feelings of *dread and awe* may be experienced. This is different from fear and anxiety, being something much deeper, a feeling in the pit of the stomach and a sense of the reality of the situation that is very, very awe-inspiring, perhaps so deeply awe-ful that it stays but for a short time, from a few seconds onwards, but, of course, may last longer. It is a feeling that may come out of the blue, triggered unconsciously or by external events. It is a deep, almost indescribable feeling of doom, of one's smallness, one's vulnerability, one's mortality. In a sense, it is that feeling of being but a grain of sand on life's seashore, with the tide coming in. It can be a sad, bittersweet, feeling. It is a feeling that sets off thoughts about life, God, infinity, and so on.

If *acceptance* appears to happen immediately, it may be covering deeper, more painful feelings and is not genuine acceptance.

Acceptance rarely happens immediately and may never happen totally. Ideally a person should reach a stage of good-enough acceptance, meaning that she accepts that she has a disease or disability, has come to terms with other emotional reactions, and has adjusted her life accordingly. Too quick an acceptance may mean she does not fight to sustain the most optimal healthy and happy life as possible. Too much concentration on fighting the physical problems may mean she is trying to deny the presence of the illness. A good-enough acceptance means achieving a balance between coping with the illness on a daily basis and realistically accepting the limitations it imposes on her lifestyle. A person who began by asking, "Why me?" may be able to reach the point of saying, "Why not me?"

If acceptance does occur quite quickly and if it seems to be a total acceptance, this may be for the following reasons. The patient or client may be reacting according to indoctrinated religious beliefs that she has accepted without thought. A patient who has had a life-long depression, maybe a "smiling one", not acknowledged by her, and with an unconscious death-wish (the causal factor to do with her early relationship with her parents), may accept her diagnosis readily. The illness may also serve a function for the patient, providing secondary gains, such as the attention never before received, and so such a patient may accept a diagnosis relatively readily.

However, real acceptance of the diagnosis that a person has a disease or disability occurs when the other stages of feeling, thought, and emotion have been gone through, when the patient has acclimatised to her new life and has found successful and positive ways of coping. Even so, there will be regression on occasions to previous stages for varying reasons—perhaps because a particular stage has not been completed, perhaps because of the effect of recurring or new symptoms later in her life which necessitate the need to go through the stages again, albeit more quickly. Grieving is the emotion an ill person is most likely to return to, as with grieving for a lost loved one, and also, perhaps, to feelings of horror and dread.

If the illness is one that usually proves fatal, then good-enough acceptance will include coming to terms with the idea of one's death, one's fears about it, one's fears for the family and friends left behind, plans for and putting one's affairs in order when and if necessary.

In conclusion, the emotion reactions to receiving a diagnosis are similar, if not the same, to those reactions a person goes through in the stages of grief. This is because basically he or she is grieving for the loss of the life and health he or she was used to, knew, and understood. There is much written about the stages of grief—for example, by Colin Murray Parkes (1972) or Lily Pincus (1974).

CHAPTER THREE

Living with a life-threatening tumour: in search of meaning and creativity

Dorothee Steffens

This is an account of a young woman's ongoing struggle to come to terms with the premature confrontation with her mortality: her search for meaning in what seems meaningless and incomprehensible, to find hope in the face of hopelessness, to risk living instead of just surviving. This painful process involves explorations on many levels, conscious as well as unconscious. The central issue, however, is the need to make sense of the profound changes in her internal as well as her external world.

* * *

Eight years ago, when she was 28, Beth suddenly started to have headaches. As she led a full life (she had just started a successful practice as an aromatherapist), she ignored these at first. When they got worse she consulted her doctor, who suggested ordinary headache pills. Although nothing brought her any relief, nobody seemed to take these persistent headaches seriously, least of all Beth herself.

After about three months, her condition had deteriorated so much that she spent most of her time in bed. She had to give up work and withdrew more and more into herself. When she did go out she must have behaved so bizarrely that people thought she was on drugs. Beth has no recollection of this. All she can remember of those last few weeks is the excruciating pain and pressure in her head. (Doctors later confirmed how close to death she had been.)

Finally, a friend realized how ill she was and took her, there and then, to the nearest A&E hospital. For the first time she was given a scan which revealed a tumour (meningioma) of the size of a grapefruit in the centre of her brain. She immediately had surgery to relieve the pressure on her brain. As the tumour was so big, she required a second operation eight weeks later, and a third one fourteen months later. After the last operation, an angiogram revealed that the tumour was inoperable and therefore permanent, as its roots were too deeply and inaccessibly lodged in the brain. At the same time, an acoustic neuroma was discovered behind her left ear that so far has been left untouched. This third operation was followed by six weeks of intensive radiotherapy.

* * *

Beth's prognosis is uncertain: she lives from six-month period to six-month period, when she has check-ups and scans to monitor the growth of the tumour(s). Any operation now could mean permanent disablement, a stroke, or even death. Beth feels that it is like living with a "time bomb", a "ball and chain", a "life sentence". She has not been able to go back to work, receives benefits, and has been given a small flat in a housing association. She has loyal friends, but ultimately she leads a solitary and lonely life—a painful contrast to her life before her illness. As she needs her friends it was painful for her to discover how angrily envious she is of all of them: their lives go on, they work, have partners, have babies—everything she feels deprived of. She keeps these feelings well hidden from her friends in order not to be a burden to them or alienate them. Her parents live in another part of the country. They are supportive yet defend against their own helplessness and grief by pretending that Beth is "fine". Beth colludes with this, as she feels that her neediness and vulnerability would be too much to bear for her parents.

Three years ago, Beth was referred by her doctor to our service. When we started to work together, meeting once a week, she was severely depressed and on antidepressants. Fairly soon into our work, she decided to stop taking them, as she felt they numbed her feelings. To make sense of what had happened to her, she needed to identify her feelings and find a language for them in order to reintegrate them into her conscious self. She began to discover the extent and depth of her impotent rage and grief that this should have happened to her. At the same time, there was a sense of deep guilt and being punished for some wrongdoing. On a more primitive level, she associated this with her having left home and started a separate and independent life of her own. These feelings needed a container, as initially they felt uncontrollable and overwhelming. Fortunately, Beth had had several sessions of art therapy at the Royal Marsden Hospital before she came to me, which had helped her to express some of her more persecutory internal experiences through painting and thus to transform them into more meaningful, almost archetypal, images. As she found this process helpful, we continued to make it part of our work together. We discovered together, over time, that her illness had reactivated many feelings and reopened old wounds from the past that had been successfully defended against or even repressed. This painful task of making sense of it all was facilitated by her ability to produce fantasies as well as many paintings and drawings stimulated by her illness. It allowed us to gain a deeper understanding of her internal world and its unconscious contents.

* * *

What had happened to Beth was a traumatic shock to her psyche. As with any trauma, we began our work with talking through Beth's experience: what it had felt like when she first felt ill, her sense of abandonment and isolation during the three months leading up to her first operation; the impact of the operations themselves; her initial elation, almost euphoria, after the operations, being without pain again, being the centre of attention, feeling almost reborn. The initial period of getting better gave her life a focus, a kind of meaning, it felt to her like going uphill towards a goal. Yet once the physical wounds had healed and she became physically stronger, the reality had to be faced of living with this "thing" and the profound and irrevocable changes it had caused in her life. To her this felt like moving downhill towards some inevitable catastrophic outcome. She saw death, at this point, as the least-feared possibility; in fact, she sometimes thought almost enviously of those who had preceded her: they were safe and released, whereas she still had to struggle daily with the certainty that death would happen and the uncertainty of not knowing when. She felt fragile, vulnerable, empty, and trapped.

The painting in Figure 1 highlights the degree of regression after the illness: her vulnerability, her inability to articulate her feelings, as well as her sense of loss of self. The feelings of entrapment, symbolized by the triangular shape, can also be linked to oedipal issues, her internal entanglement with her parents, which were to reappear more noticeably in a later painting (Figure 3).

The unbearable or unthinkable was expressed at first in quite simple, colourful, almost abstract, shapes. Reflecting on these enabled her to gradually develop a relationship with her illness and

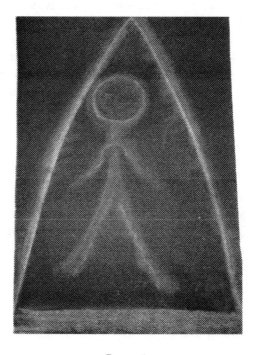

FIGURE 1

to put into words how annihilated she felt by her illness, how the tumour had robbed her not only of her youth, but also of her identity as she had known it. It felt to her as though the illness had ripped out her old self and put in an unknown mad self that created internal chaos. She was filled with fears that the tumour would become her sole identity, that in future she would only be seen by others in terms of her illness. At the same time it hurt and angered her that once the physical scars had healed and her hair had grown back, people's initial interest and concern gave way to what felt to her like unawareness or even denial of the seriousness and permanence of her physical condition.

This led to the exploration of her own changed relationship with her body and the role the tumour plays in how she now perceives herself: before the tumour, she took her beauty for granted and had no inhibitions in showing off her body. Her pride and joy was her hair: a long mane of henna-coloured wavy locks, somewhat evocative of a pre-Raphaelite beauty. She had endless energy and would set off on adventurous trips on her own, confident in being able to face any crisis. She had had relationships, although they had all been somewhat unsatisfactory, with difficulties around dependence and commitment.

Since the operation, Beth feels much more uncertain about her body. Although she is still very beautiful, willowy, and tall, she is conscious of wanting to hide her body, afraid of being seen. This seems like a paradox, as she has a striking way of dressing: colours and textures are put together in such a way that it is a visual and aesthetic pleasure to look at her. Her hair has grown back, but now has a different quality—much softer, finer, and thinner. Her hair mostly hides her enormous scar and very slight deformity at the top of her forehead. She always wears either a headscarf or a knitted cap. The overall impression is individualistic and stylish. It took Beth a long time before she could take off her head coverings and let me see her scar. The scar is her physical area of shame, and it is accompanied by fears of ridicule (i.e. having to reveal it to a hairdresser and arousing disgust or pity). It is as though the scar did not just represent an external damage, but allowed people to see her internal imperfection.

* * *

It was interesting to observe how Beth's paintings and drawings enabled her to reconnect with her feelings on several levels: sensual, aesthetic, erotic, and aggressive. Most of this had been acted out before her illness in rather unconscious ways. The tumour appeared in many different guises in her paintings. Thinking and talking about the images revealed how identified Beth had become with the tumour. It filled her being like a tyrannical baby with a voracious appetite. To keep this baby satisfied meant, on an unconscious level, to sacrifice her own separate life. As we explored the symbolic meaning of the tumour, Beth felt that the tumour, on a deeper level, represented her own voracious, aggressive, and split-off baby needs and has become a hook for already existing unconscious fears surrounding separateness and autonomy. It is easier to blame the tumour when she feels she is standing still: her fantasy is that the tumour will enviously retaliate and grow if she experiences any excitement or passion, creatively, sensually, or sexually. She fears that any of this would be "bad" for her. This "badness" feels catastrophic and irreparable.

As a result, her life has become boring, predictable, and over-cautious. She feels increasingly that she is doing the "right" thing for the tumour, but the "wrong" thing for herself. Internally, it makes her feel more and more inauthentic, unreal, and unalive. Doing the "right" thing is playing it safe, where nothing changes. She longs for change, yet change, we discovered, is associated for her with loss, separation, and abandonment. The resulting inner tension makes her feel hot, dizzy in her head, exhausted, and frustrated (Figure 2). She feels that the tumour absorbs all her energies. "How can I have a relationship with anyone if the tumour dominates me so? There is no room for anyone else."

Facing these conflicts enabled her to get in touch with much more unconscious parts of herself: a ruthless, hungry, and passionate part, filled with a murderous rage that has been repressed since early childhood. Exploring this uncovered that this part is associated with the 2-year old toddler. When Beth was that age, her mother was diagnosed with TB and sent to a sanatorium for three months. Beth, who had been a lively and happy infant, accustomed to much attention as the youngest of three, became extremely defiant and given to terrible temper tantrums after her mother's

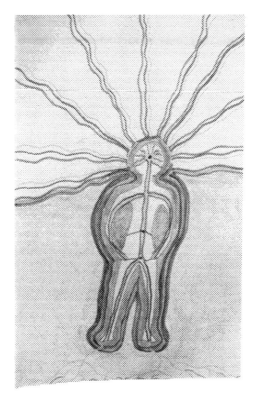

FIGURE 2

return. This lasted for a few years, and from the age of 7 or 8 she became very "good". "Good" meant undemanding and accommodating. As she grew up, she preferred to stay at home—a good safe place to be. She can now be consciously in touch with how cautious and seemingly self-sufficient she had been, even then, afraid of too much stimulation and excitement. Excitement meant desire, wanting something passionately, being selfish, becoming separate, forgetting about the parents. Being "good" meant remaining a good child who keeps the parents alive and together.

Initially, Beth called the drawing in Figure 3 "Adoration": two adoring parents protectively enveloping an infant. Behind them, a crowd of shadowy figures can be seen, associated with the external

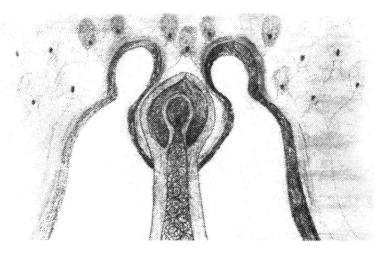

FIGURE 3

world. But they are completely disconnected from the three figures in the front, barely visible. I felt that the drawing had a certain idealizing quality. I encouraged Beth to let herself get into the drawing, and as she did so, she suddenly came up with the word "suffocation". This created a very different meaning: the infant may be protectively surrounded by the adoring parents, but it is also so deeply "rooted" in the parents that separation seems to be impossible. The parents are equally inseparably attached to their infant. This could be linked to her need to protect her parents from their fears of abandonment and loss by remaining their child who will never grow up and disappear, let alone die. Linking it to the tumour produced thoughts around the primitive control that is attributed to the tumour: the parents—or, in this case, the creative parts of her—are prevented from coming together and from engaging in a creative, internal "intercourse", as they are rigorously and "safely" kept apart by the baby/tumour. It seems clear that this joint threesome also fulfils a survival function. Another striking feature is how asexual and empty the "parental" figures appear to be. We understood this drawing to be an unconscious, defensive reaction to Beth's attempts to separate herself from early, outlived primitive behaviour patterns as well as from the control of the devouring baby/tumour. This has become the leitmotiv of our continuing work: how to give the tumour a space that realistically acknowledges its presence and power in Beth's life without allowing it to devour her life or having to sacrifice a separate identity in order to prevent the tumour from growing.

* * *

More recently, Beth had two dreams that seemed to be a continuation of the underlying themes of this drawing.

First dream:

"A warm, sunny Mediterranean landscape—she is running through a cornfield and savouring the feeling of physical freedom. Suddenly, she is bitten by a snake and quickly has to be dragged away. She feels poisoned, drained of all energy."

This dream seems to represent Beth's longing for sensual, erotic, as well as creative, freedom. The snake, however, seems to symbolize her split-off, unconscious, aggressive, and sexual energies and her fantasy of their (self-)destructive power.

Second dream:

"She finds herself in a crooked red house. It is completely boarded up. She manages to open it up and let in warm sunlight. At the same time, she is aware of another benign presence in the house."

We explored this dream in terms of her sense of entrapment through her illness and the way in which it has not only distorted her sense of body self, but also inhibited her passionate and sexual self. The benign presence that helps or encourages her to open the windows and remove the boards (i.e. hard work on an emotional level) to let in light and warmth suggests a more benign and supportive internal object (an indication of her creative use of her counselling experience).

These two dreams were the precursor of a growing ability to confront her anxieties about her future, as well as her rage and frustration at the stuckness of her life. Letting herself think about what she wants to do with her life provokes another frightening image: the tumour feels to her like the head of the Medusa, and she is paralysed by its power, unable to move. This image is associated with the fantasy that if she ignores its power, it will destroy her. Yet, as in the myth, she has to find a relationship with the tumour that will not destroy her. This fantasy is compounded by the fact that the tumour has begun to grow again, although there is no indication at what rate it is growing. On a more primitive level, Beth feels that this is a punishment for having paid too much attention to her own life and needs (a negative projection on the counselling process).

Dealing with this conflict arouses powerful survival fears; it is either her life or the life of the tumour—as though coexistence or a relationship between her disabled and healthy parts were impossible or even forbidden. It is an act of courage and a leap of faith for Beth to take more risks in terms of venturing into the unknown in a more symbolic and creative way than before her illness. This will mean tolerating frustration, sadness, and disappointments when her plans don't quite work out as she had hoped or when her body lets her down by not providing the energy she needs. However, this process also provides her with the opportunity to integrate her illness more into her life and to discover that she does have hidden sources of creative energy from which she can draw. There is a growing sense that she can emerge from the sense of panic that grips her when faced with change or loss of control.

* * *

This painful and difficult process of trying to reconnect with herself has given Beth the courage to enrol in a couple of evening classes, not only to pursue and develop her considerable artistic talents, but also to strengthen the resilience of her body.

She has often reflected on the almost total lack of support groups for people like her and, as a result, has more recently enrolled in a counselling course that she hopes will enable her to use her experience of living with a life-threatening illness to help others in a similar situation. This venture confronts her with unfamiliar challenges and pressures: academic work and rivalry and competitiveness within a group. She is greatly troubled by this and afraid that she might not be able to cope with it all—intellectually, emotionally, and physically. To avoid this conflict, she is tempted to withdraw into the victim part of herself identified with the illness and thus sabotage any progress and change. In moments of uncertainty, the vulnerable part of herself needs to create certainty in order not to get hurt, even if it is a negative certainty. We have discovered that at the heart of this lies the fear of being overwhelmed by and unable to cope with the violent emotions that might erupt in her if she is faced with something outside her control.

Beth cannot yet quite trust that her internal world is not all bad and spoilt and that there is a wealth of creative potential from which she can draw. Her struggle continues to come to terms with her illness and to explore and develop herself creatively, emotionally, and sexually, but in more authentic ways than before her illness. Like all struggles, it will be accompanied by disappointments and heartaches, as well as by triumphs.

CHAPTER FOUR

Avoiding the issues: the consequences of poorly managed diabetes

Susan Berger

L ife is uncertain and unpredictable. The way in which we deal with the uncertainty and difficulties that present themselves is often the work of therapy. This struggle with uncertainty and unpredictability was in the forefront of the difficulties presented by Marc, a 33-year-old male suffering for most of his life from childhood-onset diabetes. The details of Marc's initial assessment are described in chapter 1 ("Mr M"). He came into counselling with severe physical complications, including the beginnings of kidney failure and diabetic retinopathy (partial-sightedness). This resulted from his diabetes being poorly managed, necessitating ongoing and increasingly complicated medical intervention, culminating in a renal transplant. His life had become a series of medical appointments against the backdrop of an existence bereft of close human relationships. He had very little social life and drifted from job to job about every eighteen months.

Alongside his physical problems, Marc had suffered from depression for years. At one level, his depression was closely connected to his illness. However, Marc was aware that this was too simple an explanation for how he was feeling and the difficulties he was experiencing. He was very keen to engage in ongoing work to begin to explore his inner world in more depth while, at the same time, having to deal with the physical realities of his illness—an illness that was both chronic and progressive. It had become a lifelong companion, potentially life-threatening and closely entwined with his sense of identity. The possibility of dying was, and is to this day, an ever-present reality.

From this position, we began a journey together. I found Marc to be very charming and personable, with a delightful and endearing disposition. It felt very easy to engage with him. Over the course of three years, Marc attended his sessions on a weekly basis, but with increasingly long absences due to a combination of his failing health and his attempt to maintain a job as a director of a charity. From the outset, he showed a positive regard for the sessions as a containing, reliable space where he could begin to explore his feelings and fantasies as well as confronting the reality of his illness, in the context of a dependable relationship. Sometimes he would comment that he felt that he lived for his sessions, often announcing that he was pleased to be here after yet another difficult week. It seemed that the one predictability was the way the sessions would begin: with a medical update that was always detailed, showing a sound grasp of what was going on for him physically. This was the reality of his life, a reality that took over from everything else and ensured that any idea of a "normal" life had to be abandoned. It also conveyed how Marc's sense of himself and his identity was closely bound up with his physical illness. Marc acknowledged that he felt that it was his illness that made him an interesting person.

Background

Marc was one of four children. He has an older brother and sister and a younger sister. They grew up as expatriates in East Africa. Marc experienced his father as regimented and controlling, unable to confront or deal with difficulties. He was a bully at home. Marc described how the house would fall silent as his father's car approached the house and the engine stopped. The family would "freeze" in anticipation of his impending arrival. Marc recalled how his father would comment on how "my kids always let me down" and how they "are all a disappointment". To this day, Marc is filled with anxiety at the idea of confronting his father in any way, and the sense of futility and impotence he grew up with still undermines him. Marc described his mother as an alcoholic who was largely ineffectual. His parents met through an amateur dramatics group in former Nyasaland—and family life for Marc has been like watching a play, or rather a melodrama, that features a dysfunctional family who appear to behave like a set of strangers.

Marc's primary attachment in childhood seemed not to be to his parents but more to the country he grew up in—the landscape and feel of Africa, the archetypal earth mother. He received more care from the servants than from his parents whom he experienced as distant. The idea of distance became concretized when he was 10 years old and was sent to boarding-school in England—a cold, dark, foreign land—where he was left to his own devices. Marc recalls stealing money at school, but in such a way that he could easily be found out. He sees this very much as an enactment in order to receive attention from those around him.

A notable event that took place during Marc's childhood was the experience of being sexually abused on one occasion by a family friend. The fact that the abuser was a doctor has had profound implications for Marc's encounters with the medical profession throughout his life. In addition to this, Marc was devastated by his parent's reaction to this event when he told them about it. They took no action, as they wanted to avoid what they felt was a difficult and embarrassing situation. Marc's experience of authority figures in his life has been epitomized by their failure to meet his emotional needs, their distance, and their apparent lack of care.

Development of the work

Marc's depression was connected both to his illness and to his lack of sense of self as someone independent of his illness, as an effective, relational human being. The depression prevented him from engaging with life in a satisfying way. How Marc functioned in other areas of his life, apart from his illness and hospital appointments, constituted an important part of the work. Marc had tended to change jobs on a frequent basis. He had recently started a new job as a director of a charity but was not particularly enjoying it. I explored the possibility of Marc taking antidepressants to help him function in his daily life. Marc responded positively to this suggestion and was referred to a psychiatrist. The antidepressants, together with the therapy, seemed to work well for Marc. He started to engage in a very positive way with his work, to enjoy it, and to feel connected both to what he was doing and to the people around him. It was truly remarkable how he carried on working despite seriously diminished energy levels and feeling extremely unwell, right up to the time of his transplant. Being able to do this represented something very positive at a time of great negativity. Marc had begun to enjoy the sense of responsibility his work gave him and the freedom he had to use this responsibility. He was beginning to experience himself as potent and effective.

Marc had lived very much in isolation. His family had always kept very much to themselves, rarely having friends. There had been little example of how to interact socially. Marc engaged in solitary pursuits—reading and computer games. He described how if someone asked him about his hobbies, he would "freeze", as he felt found out. He did not feel good enough, and he wondered why anyone would be bothered with him. I asked him if he thought I could be bothered with him. He replied with both yes and no: yes, because he was experiencing me as concerned about him in the therapeutic relationship; no, because part of him still experienced himself as not good enough to be bothered with. With the growing realization that relationships could be different, he began to engage more with those around him. He started to bring to his sessions interactions he was having with people. A woman at work opened up to him about herself; Marc told me that "I couldn't do anything for her but maybe it helped her that I listened". As Marc opened up more and more in our relationship, so it followed in other areas of his life. He began to experience himself as having something to offer, as opposed to just being someone who is "ill" that no one is interested in. Relating became a two-way process, a connection giving him an increasing sense of being alive.

A major theme of the work was Marc's experience of medical intervention and his reactions and responses to them and to those in charge of his medical treatment. One of the main difficulties that came to light was the underlying feeling that medical staff often did not know what they were doing, that they did not care, and that they were withholding information. Early in the work, Marc brought an account of how a nurse experienced difficulty in accessing a vein. Marc was furious with her ineptitude and clearly felt extremely vulnerable in what felt like an abusive situation. Marc felt powerless, just as he had always done in the context of his family relationships. While there is, of course, a reality in a less-than-perfect NHS, it became apparent that Marc's experiences had a particularly strong resonance in his childhood and did not entirely match up to the present-day reality of the situation. The earlier sexual abuse by a doctor had a profound effect on Marc's attitude towards doctors in general: he saw them as untrustworthy. This was compounded by the feeling that there would be no one there to protect him. He would often complain that "they can't get anything right" and that the problems and possible difficulties with his treatment were not pointed out to him until he discovered them for himself.

As a child diagnosed with diabetes at the age of 6, Marc was left to manage his condition. This was originally done through urine testing, then later through blood testing in order to monitor his blood-sugar levels. Marc does not ever remember being told by parents or doctors that if he did not manage his diabetes, serious complications could arise. For Marc as an adult, having to manage his condition by himself was familiar territory. His anger and frustration at those who he felt do not take responsibility was expressed in his sessions. As a child, Marc's unexpressed anger at an environment that was felt to be unsafe, uncaring, and at times abusive found expression through his rebellious act of non-compliance with his treatment plan. It was the enactment of self-harm because he felt he was left to look after himself without the support he needed and wanted from others. The external objects he experienced as damaging and neglectful became the objects of his inner world, rendering him impotent in the face of his difficulties. Marc was left with a feeling of powerlessness and futility and a sense that nothing could change. He also felt a huge sense of shame and guilt over his inability to manage his diabetes, which exacerbated his already persecutory inner world and rendered him incapable of taking responsibility for his own health. As an adult, when he encountered health professionals whom he experienced as unable to take responsibility, it seemed that they also represented that projected part of himself of which he felt so guilty and ashamed. Another ramification of his mismanaged diabetes is that it has inevitably led to further complications, thus ensuring continuing care and attention. Even if experienced at times as unsatisfactory, this was the only way Marc felt—albeit unconsciously—that he could obtain the attention he needed: through illness.

We began to achieve a clearer understanding of the unconscious processes at work affecting Marc's relationship with, and experience of, the medical profession while providing a safe containing space for Marc to start to express his anger. This seemed to enable Marc to begin to engage in a more effective way with the increasingly diverse and intrusive medical interventions. Marc began to find a voice to communicate his anxieties and his needs to the various health professionals. Sometimes his needs were heard and met and sometimes not. He was able to take greater personal responsibility for his care and to work with whatever shortcomings and imperfections he experienced in the NHS. An example of this was when he was about to begin dialysis, something he had greatly feared. He was offered dialysis at one particular hospital, which seemed to be particularly chaotic. Marc was able to request that he received dialysis at another hospital where he felt more comfortable with the care that was on offer. His request was granted, much to his surprise and delight. When he needed information, he was able to ask for it in an appropriate way rather than becoming angry and resentful. He began to work with the reality of medical care in the NHS, the problems attached to his care being divided between different hospitals and different departments—renal and diabetic. Also, the reality of having to take responsibility for himself while feeling increasingly poorly was recognized in the work as being a demanding task for anyone. The adult who was able to do this was given recognition alongside the boy who was inappropriately left to manage his diabetes for himself. Marc was no longer dominated by a sense of futility and was beginning to experience a sense of potency.

The therapeutic space became increasingly important as the one place where Marc could experience himself as whole—both body and mind—and to give meaning to those experiences. He could talk about what was happening to him physically: his sense of a gradually deteriorating body that needed more and more assistance, his increasing tiredness and lack of energy. He felt generally extremely unwell as the amount of toxins increased in his body as a result of a failing kidney. Marc underwent various surgical procedures to deal with the growing problem of access to his veins for dialysis. On one occasion, he bared his scars in a session and remarked that he felt like Frankenstein. I was able to look at his scars, feel his pain, and hear his concerns, but at the same time I conveyed to him that I experienced him as something altogether different from Frankenstein, that there was nothing repellent or non-human about him. Marc was experiencing himself as a failing body for which he felt disgust. Marc was able to bring to the sessions his fears and fantasies about his failing body, his fear of dialysis, and the fantasies about the impending transplant. What emerged in the sessions was that often the reality of his experience did not match up to what Marc had imagined. The only reliable fact was that everything was uncertain and unpredictable, not just for Marc but also for the "professionals". This, of course, included me as the therapist.

It often remained uncertain as to whether or not Marc could attend his sessions due to his physical condition and the effort of trying to maintain his job. Life was making increasing demands on Marc at a time when his energy levels were diminishing. This was a reality that had to be accommodated. When Marc first started to miss his sessions, he did so without calling to let me know. I not only experienced the uncertainty of whether Marc would be attending his sessions, but I was also left with wondering why. When I asked him how he felt about his absences, Marc revealed that he imagined I would be cross, put out, inconvenienced, and that I would respond by telling him not to bother to come. He would then have to own up to this being his fault. It did not occur to him that I may be concerned and that in fact I actually cared about him. When I asked him what this reminded him of, it became clear to him that it was as if I was his punishing, uncaring father whom he was doomed to disappoint. His appointment time was held open, but there were often long periods when Marc was unable to attend. We had agreed a fee structure of a retaining fee for the unattended sessions, whereas the attended sessions would be paid for at his full rate. He continued to find it hard to phone to let me know in advance, leaving me with the uncertainty—just as he had to live with constant uncertainty.

Perhaps the hardest uncertainty was the possibility of Marc dying. There is a significant difference at a psychological level between working with terminal illness and working with a serious illness, which may or may not result in death. With a terminal illness, there is a certainty, or near certainty, which can be worked with as something to come to terms with. In Marc's case, the possibility was constantly in the background while Marc struggled to maintain hope for a future, a future Marc very much wanted. The fear and possibility of death was named and given recognition by both of us in the sessions. For Marc, it was the way in which he might die, of which there were several possibilities, that caused him the most anxiety. The time he came closest to dying was as a result of falling down the stairs in his parent's house, a completely unexpected and unpredictable event, which had serious implications for someone in his condition.

During the course of the work and as Marc's condition deteriorated, he gained support from his younger sister. She provided the love, care, and attention that seemed to be missing. Marc felt his dependency on his sister grow, and the extent of his neediness caused him some distress. She would accompany him to his sessions when it became too difficult for him to travel on his own. I was moved by her dedication and care. Marc was able in his sessions to voice his concerns regarding his sister, as his illness was now making greater demands on her. Marc's parents, now retired and living in England not far from Marc, were often absent, unable to offer any emotional or practical support. On the rare occasions that Marc's mother accompanied him on his regular visits to hospital as an outpatient, he ended up looking after her, as she was overcome by the stress of the situation. Marc's illness was only referred to in passing by his parents, as it was something they were unable to deal with, reinforcing his sense of isolation. Marc described how his parents would offer help after the event, with them often remarking: "if only we'd known" and "we want to do our duty". When they did ask if there was anything they could do, there was always some reason that they could not manage a particular day or time.

These distant and seemingly uncaring parents were very much present in the consulting-room. Part of Marc wanted to rage against them, while another part wanted to protect them, as he would announce that "they do the best they can" and "they do try". He felt guilty about his negative thoughts and, at the same time, recognized their impotency. His conflicting feelings were given expression in the work, recognizing the validity of his anger and frustration as well as his understanding of his parents' limitations. Marc felt that his parents always wanted to put a positive light on his illness. In the therapeutic relationship, he was given a space to name and confront his fears and anxieties and to have them heard and recognized. This also helped to reinforce Marc's sense of self as a person with valid and appropriate thoughts and feelings, not just to experience himself as a body being treated for various malfunctions.

The transplant

The immediate future was uncertain. Originally, the plan was to have both a renal and a pancreatic transplant, which would have meant the end of Marc's diabetes. When we explored fantasies about a life without diabetes—which, on one level, would be a dream come true—he also came to realize that it was hard to imagine who he was without the illness. However, this scenario never came to pass, as due to the urgency of his condition he underwent a single renal transplant. This meant that he would still be diabetic and the issue of managing his diabetes would continue to be part of his life. At the time of writing, Marc is in the post-transplant period, and to date he seems to be managing his diabetes. The donor was his sister—the one person who had taken on the role of caregiver and supporter to Marc as he became increasingly debilitated. Her increasing presence and role in his life culminated in her healthy kidney replacing Marc's failing kidney. Part of her is now present in Marc's body, giving him a new lease of life, free from dialysis. Much of Marc's anxiety prior to the transplant was who would provide the care now that his main source of support would need care herself after the operation. The fact that the donor was his sister also provided Marc with an even more urgent need to survive, to make her sacrifice worthwhile.

* * *

A lack of connection was a feature of his internal world, like his disconnected family. Marc once described how he saw his flat in bits—an armchair, a television, like blocks of spotlight with the rest in darkness. In the spotlight, Marc was personable, cheerful, and coping. In the darkness, he was falling apart, full of anger, with strong, persecutory feelings and low self-esteem. Efforts to conceal what is in the darkness—or, in the Jungian sense, "the shadow"— create a tension, which can often lead to a symptom such as an act of self-harm. In the case of Marc, the symptom was his inability to manage his diabetes. Another tension was his wanting to be seen, to be recognized and noticed, while at the same time being fearful of it. Marc remarked on the "visibility" and "invisibility" of his illness. He derived some relief when he had a manifest symptom such as neuropathy affecting his arm, for which he wore a support. People could then see there was something wrong. He experienced relief when I recognized his anger. Therapy helps to cast light on the shadow. In so doing, the symptom has started to dissipate. At the same time, Marc has allowed himself to have "good objects" in his life.

As with the nurse, referred to earlier, who was unable to access a vein, the phantasy in our relationship was whether or not I could access Marc's vein. Would I be like the nurse and his parents, unable to deal with Marc? Bringing pain in therapy is central to the work. When working with physical illness, one has to deal with, and be able to tolerate, both realities while separating out the sense of self from the illness and integrating the experience of both body and mind.

When faced with Marc's reality of illness, depression, and possible death, I would often feel helpless. I also had to deal with my own feelings about parents who are incapable of offering appropriate care and concern in the face of their son's considerable suffering. I was filled with admiration for Marc, who carried on in the face of so many difficulties, and for his sister, who has shown dedication and support with love and kindness.

Since the transplant, I have visited Marc in hospital, when he was admitted with problems with the new kidney. I had also visited him in hospital after his fall down stairs, and I had planned to visit him after the transplant but, interestingly, I caught a cold, which made it impossible. The visits were important both for him and for me. He referred to the link between us through phone calls and the hospital visits as "a lifeline". Because of the reality of his illness, the therapeutic relationship needed to extend outside the consulting-room.

While examining the meaning of his illness for Marc, I also held in mind what he represented for me. This was a journey I had been on in my own life ten years earlier with someone very close to me, who suffered from a serious illness, which might have led to a transplant. When Marc announced the date of his transplant, it turned out to be on the anniversary of the death of the loved one I had lost and it was in the same hospital. I had also lived with the uncertainty and unpredictability, having to take one day at a time trying to maintain a cautious optimism while fearing the worst. Although I did not disclose my personal details, it was this experience of uncertainty that I shared with Marc, as I accompanied him on his journey, that he most valued, holding those words in his mind as he struggled to survive in a sea of uncertainty. It became clear that a psychodynamic understanding of how Marc's past relationships and his internal world affected his present-day relationships and experiences was crucial to the work. It enabled him to ask for and receive the help he needed in order to manage a life with a serious physical illness. When links were made in sessions between past and present experiences, I felt a meeting in the moment, an appreciation from Marc when light was shed on what he was feeling, so that he no longer felt alone, isolated, but was held and recognized. However, from Marc's comments, what he found to be the most helpful appears to be the understanding of the nature of the reality of his external world: how to take a day at a time and know and expect uncertainty and unpredictability. He was able to make use of the therapy to find his own personal meaning to his experiences. Both realities were realities that were recognized in the context of a relationship with, in his words, "someone who gives a damn".

CHAPTER FIVE

Living in the shadow of death

Lynda Snowdon

A number of clients who were referred to the counselling service were young men and women in early adulthood who were HIV-positive or who had already developed AIDS and therefore faced a premature death. How they managed this difficult life experience was dependent both on their inner resources and on the external support they received, including a long-term therapeutic relationship.

Chay

For those with a life-threatening condition, there is an acute realization of time past and time future: it is a time of intense reflection and introspection. The life force within has a silent companion: our birth brings death as a certainty. The foundation of self-esteem comes from the introjection of love in its fullest form, passed from parent to child at the earliest stage of self development. If a child has had good early experiences she or he is more able to manage difficult and devastating life events. For those with a life-threatening condition who have never felt a strong sense of self, an additional burden is added to the will to live.

Deeply depressed and feeling empty within, Chay, who had suffered from HIV for a few years, made the first move towards seeking help in therapy. I sensed in him the presence of a life force, unknown to him in words—a force so powerful it brought him face to face with the situation he both feared and yearned for the most: a relationship. It was my privilege to be part of what was, through the therapeutic alliance, a profound experience of re-birth—the development of a sense of self that makes possible the recognition of the other, thus opening the door to attachment.

This account covers a period of four and a half years. It describes the therapeutic process that proceeded from that powerful seed of life that forced its way to recognition. It focuses on the power of unconscious communication where emotions are deeply frozen and no emotional language exists. It shows how transference and countertransference are fundamental processes, working via the therapist for the well-being of the client.

It is within the therapeutic relationship that individuation–separation develops, the struggle for the one reflected in the struggle of the other. This account highlights the two major processes that made this possible for Chay. First, the incorporation of a sufficiently "good-enough" experience through the therapeutic alliance, and second, the resolution of the negative transference. The theories of Melanie Klein (1935, 1946) with regard to the transition from the paranoid–schizoid state to the depressive position were a constant resource for me throughout the work. As good triumphed over bad, so Chay could live life in the shadow of death. Attachment, yearned for but feared, could be experienced in the shadow of loss.

This account also highlights the power of the defences—in particular, omnipotence. It demonstrates how the emergence of the true self enabled Chay to leave his entrapping defence for the relief of being ordinary. It reveals the effect of narcissistic disturbance on the development of the self and the brittle refuge of archaic grandiosity.

Chay is an artist, a gay man in his thirties whose presenting problems concerned his need to feel and express his anger before it built up and overwhelmed him. He had a rash on his face, which flared up and embarrassed him. Chay still yearned for the long-term partner from whom he contracted HIV and who subsequently left him. As he began his therapy, his health had improved and he was able to end his first course of drug treatment. This healthy period highlighted Chay's awareness of the meaning of his condition and the emptiness he felt in life. He wanted to succeed, and felt he had not made the most of his opportunities. While HIV was not the presenting problem, it was a constant presence and became the central concern as our work progressed.

In therapy

Chay spoke freely of his early anguish. He was the middle child of three boys, and he felt both persecuted and excluded—possessions were taken from him, and he felt that love was only given to others. Life was harsh, and I felt a shiver at the rawness of his early negative experiences. The family moved home frequently, and this added to the isolation he felt. Temporary accommodation seemed to be a metaphor for his sense of self.

Chay was desperately aware of the effect of the angry mother whom he had internalized. As a child, his experience of her anger had left him "numb except for a heartbeat". Tears were inaccessible to him in this paralysed state. He yearned for the father whom he experienced as absent to him—usually out of the house and unavailable when at home.

In our sessions, Chay ruminated constantly on his lifelong efforts to get his emotional needs met by his parents, only to be disappointed again and again. He was left with acute feelings of emptiness and rage. The worthlessness he had always felt was a part of his narcissistic wound. He felt abandoned and deeply persecuted by others. He thought by giving to others he would receive something in return, but this never happened. "No one is ever there for me," he said. The original wound had been perpetuated by his persecution of himself and others. The rawness had a physical dimension—a reflection of unconscious self-hatred, symbolized by the rash and inflammation of his skin.

The paucity of good early experiences rendered Chay emotionally starved. My thoughts focused on what had been missing for him in the early formative years of child development. Kohut (1968, 1977) highlights the parental need to respond positively to the child's archaic grandiosity. He stresses the importance of the merging-mirroring-approving mother and the idealized father, as well as the consolidation of a more realistic and robust self-esteem, which develops as the child faces repeated minor disappointments in the loving care of the mother and father.

Chay's archaic grandiose self, lacking recognition and subsequent maturity, was his narcissistic protection against the worthlessness and hopelessness he felt and projected onto others. It had made existence possible, but as he was facing death, Chay had a desperate need to find a sense of life within. Individuation–separation was paramount if he was to be emotionally free to be alive in the years left to him. His omnipotent defence prevented the closeness and love for which he yearned. Could it be discovered through a therapeutic alliance that facilitated his growing self?

In early sessions he spoke of the need to move from the pull of the heroic to a more comfortable feeling. He had felt an easy target for the anger and envy of others. This, he said, had been the same for his family in each of the many neighbourhoods in which they had lived. He spoke of knowing what others were thinking as if he were inside their skin. His predictions seemed to give him a sense of control. Underlying this, I sensed his fear of chaos—the baby's raw state, where without the mother's containing care, unknown sensations are acutely felt and overwhelm. This linked, I thought, to the fear he had always felt of something dreadful about to happen. His merged symbiotic state was uneasy and exhausting but fundamental to his present existence. In the alliance, I was the other, the witness who listened and responded. It felt as if I were a witness to his existence, mirroring back his reality. I was very moved by his memories. Tears in my eyes showed that he had had an effect on me. It felt as if there was an unspoken emotional connection between us, and, in those moments, perhaps for him something real stirred in his emotional world and connected, too, with his past.

In revisiting the past, Chay was able to release some of his tension, but I was aware of his acute pain as his deeply frozen emotional world began to stir. As each session progressed, I felt a heaviness—like a dead weight. I was concerned by my powerful countertransference, which not only conveyed his sense of deadness to me, but also alerted me to the hopelessness he felt. These unconscious transmissions guided me in other crucial ways. First, containment was a priority. Second, I needed to hold the hope for him. Furthermore, I needed to be positive and to be experienced as positive—like a mother with a baby, providing a secure holding environment, mirroring back an unfolding self, mediating fears but remaining in touch with reality. I was concerned whether Chay would be able to take anything from me. In the beginning, his desperate need was a positive force. It felt as if I represented the good mother. I became idealized. Later, we were to discuss the pedestal on which he had placed me. There, I was protected from his anger and envy, but this idealization also prevented Chay from becoming dependent on me. He began a counselling-skills course, and I wondered about an unconscious negative competitive undercurrent—wanting to know what I knew, do it himself, be independent, be in my skin.

Being in a group on the skills course helped Chay to focus on the acute difficulties he had with others. He was concerned that I would be exhausted or damaged by him. He was anxious about transferring his anger of women onto me. I discussed the importance of his being able to express his anger towards me. This understanding, I think, helped him to speak of how he manipulated others. When asked, he agreed that I had also been included in this manipulation. Chay's insight became a real strength to him. As his understanding grew, he was also able to express his need of me (as a containing figure).

As he gradually became aware of my concern for him, he began to take greater care of himself and made himself more comfortable in his flat. At a deeper level, his living space was a metaphor for his creative inner space.

Chay was already becoming more aware of his anger. He feared abandonment if he expressed anger, and he feared the skin rash developing as his anger erupted. Klein's ideas concerning the origins of anger helped me to understand its significance for Chay. Klein (1957) believed that babies are born with anger and envy and that it is with the mother's love that the baby begins to tolerate and not reject parts of the self. In the absence of the mitigating mother, bad parts of the self are split off and the ego is depleted. It was important that Chay expressed his anger in a safe place. In this way, he would begin to regard it as an acceptable part of himself. Incorporated into his ego, it would give him strength and could then be used constructively. At an unconscious level, Chay was communicating his anger to others. This he had yet to discover. What he did begin to understand was how he persecuted himself, and understanding this allowed him to begin to deal with it. For the first time he faced up to his mother when she criticized his artistic potential. His anger was contained and expressed constructively.

Chay made the link between his skin rash and his angry feelings and realized that he had probably always had a nervous undercurrent. I thought about the possibility of the rash representing an attack on his skin from within, the skin as the physical container of self. The significance of the face as the visual centre of identity could not be underestimated.

Chay's internal world was changing, and so was his home. He moved from a flat that had problems that he could not rectify to one that he liked. Although this, too, needed attention, he thought it capable of repair, reflecting his developing containment within. He observed that he was more able to cope with feelings of loss. We talked of his care of himself, physically and emotionally, and what was best for him. He was the centre of attention in a real way. Roderick Peters (1991) notes the often hidden version of transference of the infantile wish for mothering or fathering in narcissistic clients. There are, he says, "enormous needs for admiration, love and reliable care" (p. 88). Chay began to realize that though he could not change others, he could change himself. He recognized how hard it was not to be pulled into destruction. This was highlighted by his continued longing for his previous relationship, even though he knew that it had been bad for him. He was beginning to make a connection between his thoughts and his emotions—the beginning of integration.

Development of the negative transference

As Chay began focusing on the darker side of himself, the therapeutic alliance came under threat. He was disturbed that others associated his rash with contamination—perhaps the badness he feared seemed verified. He began to realize he made people wary of him. We discussed how this stopped people getting close to

him—including me. In the sessions I experienced his sharp re-
plies, and he acknowledged that I had "fallen from my pedestal".
It seemed as if he was deeply immersed in his inner world where
control was central, a defence against vulnerability.

I began to feel very controlled and eventually useless. Chay had
said he felt "immobilized". Perhaps I was feeling this. However,
I sensed that there was something more powerful taking place.
It was possible that I had taken in what he had projected into
me—projective identification. In my useless state, I was aided by
the ideas of Rosenfeld (1987). These helped me to realize that the
projection into me of a hated part of himself had fused us together.
Rosenfeld stresses the paranoid anxieties that this causes in the
client, who unconsciously fears that the object (myself), now pos-
sessing his aggressive part, may retaliate. Rosenfeld's belief that
projective identification is a defence against intense anxieties and
feelings concerning envy, aggression, and separateness seemed
supportive of my thoughts that making me feel useless was a way,
too, of keeping my reality at a distance. Additionally, I wondered
if Chay was unconsciously connecting with his destructive feelings
that good never lasts, so get rid of it. When a positive experience
was offered and it was turned into a negative one by Chay, I challenged him. He understood and connected his response with the
way he twisted things. This opened the door to his understanding
of his difficulty in accepting a good experience and allowing himself to be helped.

There was now a powerful intensity in both the alliance and
Chay's developing sense of self. He had a growing awareness of
his destructiveness, and he was now focusing intently on the way
he related to others. As he questioned the ideas of others, so he
challenged me, attacking the links I made. It felt as if he was attacking the feeling state of "being understood". In my frustration
I drew on the associated experiences described by Bion (1987). His
belief that "attacks on the link originate in what Melanie Klein calls
the paranoid–schizoid phase" (p. 101) was particularly relevant.

Following a lessening of his depression Chay's creativity re-
turned, and he began to paint again after a gap of several months.
He acknowledged my genuine and realistic affirmation of him.
It was at this time that he was accepted for a Master's Degree in
Fine Arts, a major achievement on his part. However, there was

a powerful undercurrent of overwhelming weariness in his presence. I was aware at this stage that there was no creativity in the space between us—many words, but no emotional connection, possibly a negative therapeutic reaction.

Chay spoke of being "so tired of setting himself up for rejection and humiliation". I felt the dead weight of the past, present, and future and realized that I had to confront him. I drew attention to his recent lateness in coming to sessions, and he linked this to his passive aggression towards women. He spoke of weariness and of his thoughts of ending therapy, which had been around for some time. I asked why he stayed. He explained that each time he thought about ending, he discovered something more for himself. I spoke of the importance of not throwing away the good work we had done so far. More importantly, I stressed the fact that he had held on in the hope of something more positive in the future, when the emptiness of the therapy had paralleled the emptiness he felt in life. This had seemed a remarkable movement in the management of loss, confirming his growing sense of self. As he was now able to link good and bad experiences, it felt as if his ambivalence was reflected in the weariness we both felt.

Chay's deep discomfort and distress had always been there, but now it seemed that this greater awareness of his feelings and past experiences had so shocked him that there seemed no movement at all. He was immersed in emotion. The core issue was his narcissistic wound and the subsequent hatred of self and other. Both were graphically illustrated, some weeks later, in a small sketchbook he brought for me to see. Above a sketch of a severed head he had written: "a very good friend of mine". We looked at the other severed heads he had drawn. One was in a hospital bed. He was concerned by the realization that this was himself. I asked, "Perhaps I'm there somewhere too?" He agreed. I was there. As I reflected on Chay's infancy, the link to the ideas of Melanie Klein (1955) was profoundly helpful. She writes: "the breast taken in with hatred, and therefore felt to be destructive, becomes the prototype of all bad internal objects, drives the ego to further splitting and becomes the representative of the death instinct within" (p. 145). The power of Chay's rage seemed tempered by the containment of the alliance at this point. His pictorial representation seemed like a forerunner to symbolic representation.

It was now that Chay had the dream of his "inner child". "It was very young", he said, "and ashen and passed by, totally cut off". It had been so real that Chay awoke convinced it was still in the room. He was deeply shocked, and I was profoundly moved. This seemed like a moment of such powerful significance that it could mark either a turning point or an end—life or death. The tension heightened. I felt an enormous split of warmth and hopelessness. This countertransference suggested a powerful battle inside Chay between positive and negative. There had, as yet, been little creativity in the space between us. As Chay spoke of having "no sense of me inside", I thought about his internal world where few good memories existed. Chay had never felt the child's healthy narcissistic buoyancy of which Kohut writes, the sense of self as separate, loved, and loveable.

In the undercurrent of the battle of good and bad, I was concerned about Chay's rage that had been contained but not allowed expression. As I reflected on his words that he had "no sense of me inside", I felt his powerful resistance and the passive aggression he had feared expressing towards me. I found very helpful the understanding outlined by Neville Symington (1993) for a situation such as this. He asks: "What is the rationale for this hatred? It is simply that there is an other. In narcissistic illusion there is no other, there is only me" (p. 86). I sensed an emotional connection between us for the first time. It seemed that connection with Chay could only take place via the negative feeling (the Bad Mother), with the possibility of hate opening the door to love. Now in our struggle there seemed a separateness, with destruction at its centre. Chay wanted to end the therapy. I expressed my strong belief that this was not the time to end.

The negative transference was now faced in reality. Chay was feeling very depressed, with no hope for the future. He spoke of his neighbour, the woman upstairs, who had not been in for him when he needed her. Now, he said, he did not want her. I said, "Perhaps that is how it feels sometimes with me, that I am not there for you and part of you wants to kill me off." "I'll go with that," he said. I spoke of our struggle in sessions over the last weeks. I had disappointed him and linked this to the space between sessions, asking if it felt as if I became lost to him between them. He agreed. We focused on the change that was taking place in the therapy—two separate people alive and able to express themselves. Chay said: "Without this happening between us, nothing would have changed." It felt as if we had experienced the ego-to-ego contact that occurs in particular movements in analysis of which Symington (1986) writes and which he suggests "is a revolution because new reality, new growth begins" (p. 268). Chay had expressed his anger, and there had been no retaliation. He realized he had a choice. This was about moving from deadness to life, in the alliance and in himself.

Life or death?

During the therapy, Chay had tried four drug combinations. Each had been rejected by his body. Now he was shocked to discover that his immune system had "collapsed". His medical consultant told him it was imperative that he tried a fifth option and that it worked. This would dramatically affect his prognosis and increase life expectancy. The reality of this challenged his still maturing emotional state, but he was strong enough to meet the challenge and began the new treatment. Chay was pursuing life. As he thanked me for my help at this time I saw a glimmer of a benign object. Heimann (1952) indicates the importance of this: "the kind super-ego (the benign internal objects) acts as a spur for ego development and enables the ego to expand and venture forth" (p. 138). I had constantly been concerned for Chay's physical well-being, but now, as the weeks passed, I became very concerned about his physical weariness. He looked increasingly frail, and his pallor indicated his exhaustion. His reaction to this particular drug was taking its toll. I was very relieved when he decided to go into hospital for recuperation and assessment for future treatment. He allowed himself to be looked after and even asked his neighbour for help with his shopping when he returned home.

I was slowly becoming visible to him as a person—a triumph for him of reality over phantasy. He was beginning to realize my symbolic representation in his inner world. He accepted that there might never be a resolution with his parents, but the critical internal figures were becoming less severe. Chay had recently noticed some concern from his mother, and his father had seemed more aware of him as a son. He recognized his parents' limitations and was more able to be open to the reality of some effort on their part. He knew he would always feel a need, but he knew, too, that he could manage it—a powerful comment on his ego strength, the mediator within.

Now, wanting life, he was in touch with his birth and his struggle for life which had developed into omnipotence. Letting go of this defence in spite of its limitations was exceedingly hard to do. Over many months, he had begun to realize that his omnipotence had been exhausting, acutely uncomfortable, and unproductive. His sense of self was developing, strengthening, and based in reality. Thus he began to let himself experience the acceptable feelings of ordinariness. He was experiencing the content of being part of a group. He did not have to prove anything; he could just be, and let others be. Through the alliance, Chay had experienced the caring and affirming reflecting back of his self. In addition, he had faced reality, the disappointments and challenges in life. My idealized self was moving towards being good enough. His skin rash, he said, had become unimportant to him—"what would be, would be". Energy was more available to use constructively. He was beginning to see and accept the mixture of strength and weakness in people—an integration that reflected his own development towards an integrated inner world. His dream of being in someone else's clothes and the accompanying discomfort seemed to indicate his growing comfort in being himself—in his own skin. People who had not seen him for some time noticed the difference, he said.

In hospital he had felt so ill that it seemed he might die. To try to prepare himself, he had reflected on his life now. He was surprised to realize that although he had not fulfilled his life's intentions, he was now very happy in the knowledge that he had done his best. Chay had recognized that his life had value. In a later session he said: "Now that I have found happiness I am content to die." This realization of life brought him face to face with the reality of his death and, at times, total despair.

Chay told me that his depression had turned into sadness. His despair seemed like a deep mourning for the lost years. I was very moved as he suffered the acute sadness of potential loss of life. However, through this he was able to find his way ahead—death is a reality, but life is to be lived. He had needed to change his drug therapy and had the choice of the only two remaining options. He chose the best combination. "In order", he said, "to complete my MA and train to teach art."

Very occasionally there can be a time when the choice is made to step outside the framework of the working alliance. As we reached the end of our time together, Chay asked if I would attend his professional exhibition. After much deliberation and with the agreement of the supervision group, I decided to attend. His style seemed very different from the photographs I had seen of his earlier work. Then, vibrant colour had been contained by a frame. Now the content seemed to hold the tension, the creativity an expression of the energy. Large exhibits were entitled "Intervention". The soft muted colours, which combined two- and three-dimensional representations, had depth and substance. Circles were central, suggesting movement.

Chay directed my attention to the colours he used in exhibits of small circles, saying how he realized that they were the colours in a brooch he had made for me when we began our work. Now I reflected on the circle—the beginning and end uniting our alliance and his life. I told him of my pride in his achievement. The work and the meeting place seemed to verify our coming together and our separateness. In that moment, there was a transferential feeling of mother and son. But we were now going our separate ways. This was echoed in our next session, when I asked his permission to write his story for this book. He was moved by this request. After giving permission, he spoke of my presence at the exhibition. Pointing to himself he said: "you are alive in here." Winnicott (1971) writes that trust is where "the individual experiences creative living" (p. 103).

The attachment Chay yearned for he had allowed to develop, experience, and acknowledge. The closeness that he had allowed himself to enjoy in the alliance was paralleled in his embrace of life, whatever it would bring. His exhibition included a two-coloured neon sign entitled "Live in the Moment". He commented on the importance of this and reflected on its connection with our work, where "living in the moment" had been a constant and central theme.

CHAPTER SIX

"A journey of a thousand miles begins with the first step" Chinese proverb (attributed to Lau Tzu)

Lavinia Chant and Rosemary Dixon-Nuttall

The journey

"Don't walk in front of me, I may not follow. Don't walk behind me, I may not lead. Walk beside me and just be my friend." So wrote the French novelist, playwright, and philosopher, Albert Camus. What is friendship? Is it having someone to whom we can talk without being judged? Someone who accepts our human frailties because they understand their own. Someone with whom we can not only agree but comfortably disagree. Or is it someone, as the English philosopher and statesman Francis Bacon expressed, "to whom you may impart griefs, joys, fears, hopes, suspicions, counsels, and whatsoever lies upon the heart to oppress it . . .". Friendship, it would appear comes in many guises. But perhaps it may be summed up in even simpler terms—as someone who cares. Friends are rare. But no matter for how brief, or long, a time they walk beside us, our lives will be touched by them until we die.

Today, sitting here trying to narrate this story, I am reminded of a person who has not only been by profession a skilful therapist, but also a woman who for eleven years I came to think of as a friend. A friend who "walked" beside me and listened to me, throughout some of the most difficult years in my later life. I believe it was the Austrian-born US psychologist Bruno Bettelheim (1980) who said: "in order to survive a person needs to know that he or she is important to someone, that somebody cares very much about them." Rosemary was a caring psychotherapist, while also fulfilling the definitions given by both Camus and Bacon as to what makes a friend. In her professional capacity, she worked alongside me, through years of painful struggle, helping me to attain some semblance of peace from my terror-ridden world. Her support, offered always with quiet calmness, was continuous, as we set out together on a journey to regain my mental health.

We had our first meeting, at the William Kyle Centre of the Westminster Pastoral Foundation, on Friday the 12th of October, 1990. We were to have our last session at WPF at the end of July 2001. I went into that first meeting in the October, feeling very apprehensive. Electing to participate in therapy for a second time was a big decision on my part—a decision fraught with many misgivings. My fears and doubts, in the main, came about because two years earlier I had experienced eighteen months of difficult, unsatisfactory, and totally unproductive outpatient treatment, when attending a large psychiatric hospital in London. There, the sole emphasis had been on medication, with no psychotherapy being offered as additional support. Upon the treatment's abrupt conclusion, my former GP attempted to put me in touch with a private therapist. She, however, after discussing my case with him, elected not to see me as a client, stating that without appropriate backup she considered me to be too ill to work with at the time.

A few weeks after this occurred, I happened one afternoon to be listening to the radio when a series began, entitled "Room To Talk. Room To Listen." As I recall, it ran for six weeks and dealt with the topic of counselling and psychotherapy. A number of psychiatrists, psychologists, psychotherapists, and counsellors participated, speaking about their work and what it entailed. They discussed the choices available to people seeking therapy and what to look for when choosing a therapist, as well as the institutions that existed where such help could be found. It was during this programme that I heard about the WPF. Thus it was that, with a mixture of trepidation, despair, and courage, I contacted WPF. Some time later, after a preliminary assessment interview, an appointment was arranged with a therapist, leading to that twelfth day in October when Rosemary and I met for the first time.

It is necessary here to digress a little and explain that this was not, however, my first introduction to psychotherapy. That had taken place twenty-six years earlier in America, when I was 31 years old. In the late 1950s I had emigrated to the United States, married an American I had met in Paris, and settled down to life in Southern California. Two years later, in 1960, I gave birth to a son. Almost five years passed before I became seriously ill with what was to be diagnosed as schizophrenia. During the next six years I was admitted to hospital on three occasions. Throughout that entire period I was treated by a young psychiatrist named Tom, who was not all that many years older than I at the time. He had, however, studied, trained, and worked under the tutelage of the American psychiatrist Karl Menninger. Tom was my introduction to therapy, and he warned me at the outset that the whole process meant undertaking a lot of hard work. When Tom died in 1976 of a sudden, massive heart attack, he left me fortified by twelve years of intensive psychotherapy, and with sufficient emotional resources intact in order to cope. And cope I did. Of course, there were certain restrictions and limitations imposed by the illness and there were times when I faltered. But with medication and under the watchful eye of a family physician, who had known Tom, I lived my life. Then, an event took place of such significant magnitude that it caused my emotional Richter scale to register 10! In 1985, when I had spent nearly thirty years in the United States, my husband retired. Upon doing so he made the totally unexpected, and for me alarming, decision that we should leave California and go and live in London. For many reasons I did not want that to happen. Nevertheless, in May of that year, to my dismay I found myself flying the 6,000 miles back to a vastly different country from the one from which I had chosen to depart all those years before. My mind struggled to make sense out of the turmoil but, being fragile and vulnerable at the best of times, it began bit by bit to disintegrate. In the ensuing months, and for a devastating period of around four years, I held on—by what felt like my fingertips. Until finally, that morning of the 12th of October, 1990, I ended up in a small room at WPF sitting opposite a woman called Rosemary.

There I sat and, with a sense of hopelessness, wondered whether I could summon enough energy, either emotionally or physically, to work once more with another therapist, knowing, as I did, all that it would involve. On that morning, now more than eleven years away, I was overwhelmed by sadness—a sadness brought about, in part, by the fact that signs of my illness were breaking through again.

What was it like to work at therapy once more? Well, as I think back, embarking on that form of treatment for the second time (with someone completely different) was, for me, akin to setting forth on yet another long, exhausting journey, but accompanied this time by a stranger. As it transpired, it was to be a journey that involved thousands of miles—and one in which I again started out encumbered by a large, heavy suitcase. Along the way, some of the territory I traversed was known to me. But much of the ground covered was unfamiliar and unexplored. There were untold moments when fear of both the known and the unknown engulfed me, as, in despair, I began to travel those miles. By contrast, therapy, I decided, was rather like trying to peel an enormous onion, piece by piece, down to its core. It was a task that had to be approached carefully and cautiously. And it was a slow, oft-times painful procedure that caused much discomfort and many tears before that vital, inside kernel was laid bare and revealed. Then, and only then, was there any relief.

That October 1990, for the second time in my life, I had reached rock bottom, and once again in desperation I sought the help of psychotherapy. But there were to be no quick-fix answers offered in that form of treatment. No magic wand was waved over my head to produce a sudden miraculous cure—a cure that would dissipate my terrors, fears, and dreads. Neither therapist, in Los Angeles or London, ever promised me a future rose garden, or intimated that upon the work's conclusion everything would go smoothly and without complications. Perhaps you are now wondering what I was searching for. In the main, I came to hope that by the end of therapy a person would emerge with deeper insights and a better understanding of herself, of her behaviour and individual qualities and traits, while at the same time having

grown stronger emotionally, and, on completion of all the work, that she would be able to say that a healthier, more proficient coping mechanism had come into effect.

Undertaking to do all that required continuous effort and involved an ongoing struggle of the greatest proportions. There were days when I felt reluctant to set foot in WPF, to enter that small room and start work. There were days when, for every step I took forward, I staggered several steps backwards. And there were days when on my journey I stumbled badly, falling into treacherous potholes strewn along the way. Although I had company throughout my travels, I had to cover those miles myself. Only I could do it. Rosemary could not undertake to walk them for me. No matter what conflicts I encountered, no matter how frustrated, confused, or tired I became, no matter how often I wanted to stop peeling the onion, I had to struggle on. It was a clear choice I finally made that Friday morning, and I kept to it. I had taken my first step when I recognized and acknowledged that I was ill. I took the second when I contacted WPF, and my third step came about when I started work with Rosemary. There were, of course, untold steps left ahead of me.

Venturing forth as I was for a second time, it also became clear to me that the therapeutic process as it unfolded needed and required two fundamental ingredients. In order to get therapy underway and for it ultimately to be beneficial and to successfully meet its aims, there had to be a good rapport between therapist and client and unreserved trust. I further realized that psychotherapy was unique, inasmuch as the relationship that developed was, by its very nature and out of necessity, almost exclusively one-sided. During our sessions, Rosemary came, little by little, to learn many intimate details about me as I sat and talked to her. I, on the other hand, learned little about Rosemary as she sat and listened. But that was the way it needed to be and had to be. I would never have "opened" up and revealed my innermost thoughts, often deeply troubling ones, without there having been a degree of anonymity regarding her.

As for trust, that again was something that had to be present. And it, too, came into the sessions gradually. Trust was an essential element. Without it there could be no disclosures, no exploring, no sharing, no getting "in touch" with feelings and emotions. Without its existence there would have been no room, and less desire, to grow and develop. Apart from those two vital components, I also once more came to know what it was like to be listened to with a completely non-judgemental attitude. This factor served at all times to both reassure and provide me with a safe outlet through which I could express myself, without the constant fear of exposure to harsh criticism, rebuke, or condemnation.

During the period I spent at WPF, I explored, investigated, and even discarded some of that heavy baggage I was hauling around. At other times, I learned to redistribute the load, so that what remained became easier to bear. And yes, all the while in spite of setbacks, I continued to peel that edible bulb, layer by pungent layer, down to its core. Throughout the eleven years, I was given not only a safe room in which to talk; I had room made for me as a person so that talk became possible.

Three years after I began sessions with Rosemary, my husband died, due to injuries incurred when he was struck by a car early one morning. He lived in a coma for a week, finally being declared brain-dead and taken off the life-support system. Amidst all the trauma and subsequent bereavement, therapy was there for me as a constant source of support. In shock, I talked time and time again about the severe injuries he had suffered. In the following months and years, weekly sessions helped me adjust to living on my own. I had never experienced a solitary existence in my life until then. From the very beginning, even before birth, I'd known what it was like to have company—for I am a twin.

It has been fifteen years now since I returned to London, eight of which I have lived alone; eleven of the fifteen were spent working with Rosemary. During those sessions I grieved over many things. I knew much of sorrow and despair; came to terms with chronic schizophrenia; fought deep frustration and major depression, and even established a mini-truce with the UK and the British weather! To my joy I also became reacquainted with my American identity, knew what it was to smile and laugh again, and learned how to be kind to myself. That small room at WPF was a sanctuary, where words of encouragement and affirmation often came my way; while outside, the campus, with its charming, fragrant garden, was a welcome respite from a bustling, hectic city. I was never quite relaxed enough to sit for long in the grounds, but I walked

its paths repeatedly, enjoying the trees and flowers and the air of tranquillity that emanated forth within its cloistered walls.

Some months after my return to England, I wrote a poem which I called "The Inward Eye". In it I expressed how I had felt on the completion of my therapy in California. I quote it now, as my story comes to an end, because many of the sentiments apply to my work in London,

Years have passed
veiling your image on life's clouded lens.
The razor edge of anguish
has lost its power to sear.
Once, sharpened steel.
Today muted rust, ageing into dullness.
No more pain.
No raw open wounds
to suppurate and bleed.
Only a scar remains,
visible to the inward eye.
A furrowed welt upon the mind
lying hard beneath the hands of time—
which echoes softly with you still . . .

"Talking" therapy, in combination with medication, has given me a life outside hospitals. That "razor edge of anguish" no longer sears to the extent it once did. Now, with assistance, it has aged into dullness. Scars do exist, still there to be found "lying hard beneath the hands of time". Some days they make their presence felt more than at others. And then, perhaps they are visible to those who have an inward eye. But echoes of what I have gained and achieved from all those years of therapy in America and England resound daily in my mind. My experience in many ways was a tale of two cities: Los Angeles and London, two vastly different places 6,000 miles apart but linked, despite that, by two very different people—Tom and Rosemary, separated by a time span of twenty-six years. These two individuals each in turn not only waited with patience for me to reveal my true self, but, more importantly, had hope for me when I had ceased to hope for myself.

Looking back, I am aware that it took courage on my part to venture forth on those arduous journeys. But I was not alone. And my thanks this day go to both companions who travelled those thousands of miles with me. My thanks for their care, their compassion, their insights and abilities as therapists. And for walking beside me and just being my friends.

The therapy

I returned to join the staff at Westminster Pastoral Foundation on the 3rd October 1990, having trained there in 1986. Lavinia was one of the first clients I was asked to see, and I remember feeling both excited and apprehensive, for I had been appointed to work both on the Serious Physical Illness (SPI) team and in the General Counselling Service. Work built up gradually, and I started meeting Lavinia on the 12th of October, 1990. Neither of us knew then that we would be working together until I ended my work there in July 2001—a very long journey indeed, as it transpired.

For the first time in my professional life as a counsellor and in the early days of psychotherapy training, I would be making active use of my knowledge and previous experience of nursing. Each of us in the team had either been nurses or had been involved in some way with the physically ill. All our clients had a severe physical illness but had come to WPF due to their psychological needs.

It had been found that if the reality of the physical illness as well as the psychological reasons for discomfort could be attended to and acknowledged simultaneously, greater benefit ensued for the wholeness of the person.

My knowledge increased greatly over the years, as did my skills. I learnt so much from being with Lavinia. I had not worked with anyone suffering with schizophrenia before, and she enabled me to develop a greater understanding of the condition.

One of the benefits of the SPI team approach was that we all had weekly supervision in one of two groups of five staff members. We presented our work rotationally, but could always have some time if we needed it. I needed to after Lavinia brought in some of her very carefully drawn illustrations of her internal world in her sixth session and asked me to keep them for her at WPF. (Some of Lavinia's drawings are shown in this chapter.) They were with us in an envelope at each session and were looked at and discussed whenever she wanted to reveal more of her internal world; this was very gradual and took a very long time.

I understood during the session at which I was shown her drawings why one or two private counsellors/therapists had told her GP that she was too ill to be seen in private practice. I felt swamped by spiders, overcome by screaming mouths and very thin emaciated babies. In many of the drawings was an all-seeing eye, which I interpreted to her as always being on the lookout for her to make a mistake, and she agreed that was so. No wonder her fear of making a mistake was so powerful. Although I felt overcome, she left feeling even more afraid, because not only had she shown me her drawings, but also I had *seen* and begun to understand them.

I was told during the next session by Lavinia that she felt she would be punished for revealing those parts of herself.

Very much later I heard how she relieved her internal pain by pushing a darning needle into her upper arm on such occasions. As a small child she had learnt to hold onto her feelings, having been punished for crying or screaming. While others in the family were very angry, she became terrified by the anger.

The garden and buildings, plus the room where we met, all became very important over these years and featured in many of our sessions. Change was very difficult: when redecorating took place, as it did, if I was able to give her advance warning of the necessity of a different room I did so, but she was very unsettled if it occurred suddenly. I would feel very responsible for something totally out of my control. I learnt very quickly how she strove to be in control all the time. Only gradually did we both learn that with her illness so much was out of her control, and I realized much later that she had never fully accepted her diagnosis. It was quite a while before I learnt that she lowered the dosage of her anti-psychotic medication when she felt taken over by the illness, and at such times she would feel very suspicious of people and events. As she learnt to trust me and I to use my instinct, I would challenge her re the medication dose and she would then admit what she was doing and say she would put the dose up again. Eventually she was under psychiatric care and I could leave that area alone, unless she wanted to tell me about situations that arose. But initially she would have nothing to do with psychiatrists, due to her very deep suspicion of them following her experiences some four years earlier following her return to London from California. She felt very let down by the lack of care she had received and dared not trust any mental health worker, doctor, or nurse. It was therefore even more amazing that she began slowly to trust me.

Lavinia showed great courage in coming to see me, an older woman, when she had had so many strong women in her early life, of whom she had been deeply afraid as a child. Her therapist in the States had been a man who had died suddenly before their work ended, some years before she moved back to England with her American husband from California. She had made contact with WPF after hearing our director being interviewed on the radio. Her assessor had been a man, and I could have been a disappointment in those early days, but we seemed to make a good-enough start for her to risk continuing. I was aware of her intense fear, but also of her determination to get help in that first session, and I was relieved when she agreed to come again.

Risk it was, for she was very apprehensive and had difficulty looking at me for some weeks. I recall her telling me of her fear of having a seizure during a session (I learnt then "that dogs have fits, humans have seizures"), for as a result of her temporal-lobe epilepsy she had several minor or major seizures at times. Up until then I had never told any of my clients that I was a trained nurse with many years of experience. I told her during that session, by saying if she did have a seizure the floor had a soft carpet and I would be there. Although she felt ill many times during our sessions, she never had a seizure during them. In fact, she missed very few sessions, and we worked together twice weekly from the ninth month, as it was felt by my supervisor that she needed more frequent work. I reduced my work two years before I finished at the Foundation, and we continued with weekly sessions until the end of my time there. Initially she found the reduction of hours difficult, but she quite liked it eventually.

She was quite fragile initially and very frightened, feeling very alone. It seemed very important that she could speak with me between sessions. Returning to England was like being in a foreign land, and one she had never wanted to live in again. It was as if she needed to touch base every now and again between our sessions. I gave her my private telephone number and then told my supervision group that I had done so. The requirement of WPF was that all messages went through Reception and were either given to each counsellor in writing or each was contacted by telephone by the receptionist on duty at the time, if necessary. However, when my supervision group heard my reasons for "breaking" the requirement, they supported my decision. I had known instinctively that she would never take advantage of me, and she never did.

It was in the third year of our work that she phoned me one day to say that her husband had been knocked down while out running early that morning on a dark January day. It was his custom to jog each day in all weathers. He was severely injured, although he had been able to speak when Lavinia reached him, having been taken by the police to a local hospital. Later he was moved to a larger hospital for observation and subsequent cranial surgery, from which he never regained consciousness. The five days that he was on a respirator in intensive care were torture for Lavinia. She was being encouraged to speak to him, and this she found very hard as the beds were quite close together. Although she spent hours with him, she found time to ring me daily, and this enabled her to talk through the happenings of the day, to some extent. Then, on the fourth day she and her son were told that there was little or no sign of brain activity. The following day, they made the difficult decision for the respirator to be turned off, following a further examination by two doctors. But because her husband had wanted his organs to be used for others, to which she agreed, the respirator was left on until that surgery was completed. She was so anxious that he should not suffer any pain that she requested an anaesthetic be administered, and the doctors agreed to this. Her husband had always been very afraid of not being able to breathe, and she was not going to let him suffer, even though it cost her a great deal of courage to voice her wish. In those early days, she found it almost impossible to stand up for herself about anything.

Never before had she lived alone, and I experienced her pain, hearing her fears and anxieties relating to her new state of life. As a twin, she had very clear early memories of feeling great concern for her brother, for whom she had always felt very responsible, even to sharing, as far as possible, his punishments when he had been naughty when they were little.

Together we looked at a checklist of things she had to do before going upstairs to bed. This eventually enabled her not to have to repeat her routine too often before she set the burglar alarm and thus ascended the stairs. But the nights were very difficult and full of very disturbed dreams when she did sleep.

As we sat together session by session reliving her dreams and her husband's injuries and subsequent death, I was drawn into her deep sadness. Silence was so important, and sometimes we sat together in a deep silence of sadness. It took as long for words to be uttered as it took for tears to flow; anger being expressed was many months away and was quite frightening to her when it was tentatively expressed by Lavinia. I would be in touch with it at times and would help her to understand the appropriateness of angry feelings, but for the most part I sat with my countertransference.

In supervision I had been encouraged to be quite concrete with her at times, and it certainly was most important and enabling for her. I had previously been involved with grief counselling, and that experience served me well during this long period of desolation.

A pattern emerged over the years of greater activity and involvement in her life during the warmer sunnier months, and a slowing down into depression during the long dark days of late autumn and winter, even though she did her best to keep as active as possible. We revisited earlier happenings in her life, and she gradually developed more trust in herself and in those around her. She wrote poetry, started drawing again, and got pleasure from her activities. But life was a struggle, and she dealt with it as she was able.

Years before she had promised herself she would never again be admitted to hospital for her mental problems. She never was during our time together, and she struggled in our sessions making great efforts to stay as well as possible and to gain more insight.

Towards the end of our work together, she gave me a spiral-bound copy of her poems and drawings, prepared by herself. I was deeply touched and full of admiration for her fortitude.

CHAPTER SEVEN

Working with dual realities: psychological and physical

Linette Hatfield

T his chapter attempts to describe the approach and techniques used in counselling clients who present with the emotional impact of a physical illness and/or a disability. Psychoanalytic theories of the psyche–soma relationship have, on the whole, addressed the approach to and the treatment of patients who present with the somatic manifestation of psychological distress (e.g., McDougall, 1989; Winnicott, 1954). There may be no difference in the severity of the physical illness or in the psychodynamic-counselling principles in practice. The intrapsychic conflicts that the counselling will aim at bringing to light so that they can be explored will be similar in physical or psychosomatic manifestations. The difference lies in the aim of the counselling, which is to support clients in adjusting to the loss that inevitably accompanies illness and disability and in finding the meaning of the illness for the client.

The psychological and the physical

Psychodynamic counselling with physically ill/disabled clients requires clinicians to understand the physical condition and how it is
likely to affect the client with whom they are working. Supervision
groups that offer the shared experience gained from working with
this client group are an invaluable source of information and support. Supervision groups at WPF have the advantage of having
several counsellors and psychotherapists with extensive nursing
experience. Supervision groups help counsellors avoid identifying
clients by their illness and/or disability or making assumptions
about a client's experience and feelings.

The aim is to help clients grieve over their lost health/function
and, when appropriate, focus on what they can do rather than
what they can no longer do. Acquiring a serious illness or disability is disorienting; the patient sees him/herself and the outside
world differently. Relationships, work, plans, and assumptions
made about the future are re-examined. Coming to terms with the
loss of health and sometimes part of one's body or body function
is a struggle. There needs to be enough ego strength to engage in
the work with a counsellor and to make that adjustment.

> A client who has suffered from a degenerative disease of the
> central nervous system for over twenty years, is now wheel-
> chair-bound, has to be moved from place to place with a hoist,
> and is fed, in part, by a tube in his stomach manages to go
> to work twice a week. He goes to the latest plays, films, and
> so forth and keeps in touch with a multitude of friends and
> relatives all over the world. This is partly possible because he
> has the financial means to pay for a carer and maintain this
> lifestyle. He uses all his resources—psychological and finan-
> cial—to carry on with his life as he had done before being
> disabled. His positive attitude has helped him to overcome
> the limitations imposed by his illness. His determination is not
> based on denial: it is a combination of his inner resources and
> long-term psychotherapeutic work.

The assessment process is important in judging the suitability of the client for psychodynamic work. Mary Pat O'Gorman

(2000) describes the positive outcome of two and a half years of psychodynamic work with a young patient with severe physical and cognitive impairment. She challenges the view that conditions such as brain damage will, by definition, affect the client's ability to work psychologically. Recent developments in the field of neuro-psychoanalysis (e.g., Kaplan-Solms & Solms, 2000) have led to the publication of exciting case studies that evidence that "mind" and "brain" work—that is, that psychotherapy and neuroscience can be integrated in the rehabilitation of some patients.

However, O'Gorman (2000) also writes that "some patients seek unconsciously to return to the situation of absolute or relative dependency. Their psychological fragility, compounded by physical frailty resulting from brain-injury, means that their capacity for self-reflection and insight has also been damaged" (p. 65).

The client's fear of fragmenting and the use of a rigid defence mechanism are a contra-indication for once-weekly psychodynam-ic work. The client will resist taking the emphasis of the session away from concrete physical symptoms, and attempts to break that resistance can lead to deep feelings of anger. Psychological work on what is going in the client's inner world is made to feel futile and an affectation.

A client who suffers from a disability acquired at birth, and who is almost blind, blocks any useful work that could be done in her sessions, by attacking any psychodynamically based interpretations and by accusing the counsellor of wanting to show off her analytic credentials. She is desperate to be helped to cope with the demands of her job and the problems in her relationship with her partner, but she constantly attacks the counsellor's thinking as irrelevant.

The assessment process is used to establish the expectations of the client. Some expectations will be unconscious and will be brought into the light with time. Some are a block to useful work. For example, a client has suffered a disabling injury as a result of an accident or medical error and is actively pursuing a financial claim for compensation. The energy and excitement are elsewhere, and it is not easy to summon up to establish a working relationship with the counsellor. There will be a resistance to going beyond the concrete legal pursuit and uncover a pre-existing and unconscious need for compensation.

Whatever the expectations, the task of the counsellor is to help the client face the reality of the illness. The phantasy that is likely to accompany some physical illness is that he or she has a psychological aetiology and therefore can be "cured" by the psychological interventions of the counsellor. The aim of the counselling is to confront the phantasy and to present reality in a way that allows the client to keep healthy defences and use them in a bid to recognize and overcome manic and destructive defences such as splitting and projection. There are, however, some exceptions: seizures, for example, are in some cases caused by underlying psychological disturbance. These conversion symptoms can be relieved through counselling, often with good effect.

> A young woman suffering from severe arthritis wanted counselling because she felt isolated and depressed. Shortly after she started her sessions, she revealed that she had applied to train as a nurse and that she was in the process of challenging the occupational health department on its doubts about her suitability for training. She struggled painfully for three years, just managed to qualify, only to reject the whole idea of practising as a nurse as unrealistic. She had felt unsupported by her parents all her life. She also felt that the doctors had not taken her seriously; it had taken a very long time for her condition to be diagnosed. Her experience of being a patient, dependent on doctors' treatment, had been disillusioning. Unconsciously, in choosing to look after patients, she was attempting to look after the ill part of herself. The support she found in her sessions was instrumental in her finding and developing a more realistic career path.

It is often assumed that if the client has been disabled since birth, the adjustment to the disability has largely been achieved and is, by definition, easier than if acquired later in life. The adjustment will depend on the way the baby was perceived and nurtured. A maladjustment by the parents to the child's disability and emotional needs is felt as a rejection. It leads to a longing for an accepting and respecting parent; when it is not found, resentment and frustration can provoke a destructively angry reaction.

A client who had acquired cerebral palsy at birth was treated by her parents as the "monster" of the family. In fact, her behaviour and relationship with the outside world reflected that internalized image. She often "loses it" when faced with the smallest of stresses. Her parents' attention had concentrated on the physical aspects of her disability and put all their efforts in "correcting" her impairments. The deep sense of having been deprived of a valuing parent means that whenever she is denied something, it feels as if she is destabilized and will fragment.

In taking into account the physical reality, one has to be aware that there will be technical differences in the counsellor's technique and method of working. The counsellor will be expected to be flexible and adaptable, but also has to guard against the pitfalls therein. Implications for the therapist in relation to flexibility and managing boundaries are explored. In some cases, the counsellor has to be prepared to see the client in the client's own home. For the counsellor, the status of the encounter is altered: the normal therapeutic setting with its formalities is replaced by a setting with social overtones, and boundaries have to be carefully negotiated. During hospital visits, which sometimes are necessary if the client cannot attend normal sessions because of an admission, the counsellor will have to be prepared for the visits to be interrupted by physical interventions from hospital staff. If a client dies while still in counselling or shortly after the end of the counselling, the counsellor will have to consider the appropriateness of attending the funeral and getting in touch with relatives. The ability to hold the boundary in unpredictable circumstances will depend on sound training and a great deal of experience.

In all areas of our work, we expect to accompany our clients through their changing circumstances. With serious physical illness, we work sometimes with degenerative conditions and are likely to deal with increasingly distressing symptoms and the constant threat of an untimely death. Advances in the medical field—for example, new drugs for HIV/AIDS, which give some sufferers a new lease of life—mean that the counsellor has to review initial assumptions and help the client adapt to new circumstances. Paradoxically, facing the possibility of a longer life and all the inherent responsibilities, such as employment and relationships, can feel daunting for someone who has worked towards accepting that he or she is dying and that inevitably he or she will come to depend increasingly on relatives, carers, health services, and state benefits. Some conditions include long periods of remission and recovery of function. In these cases, clients are faced with having to make several readjustments to their self-image.

Physical illness and disability affect interpersonal relationships. Sufferer and relatives have to find ways of coping, sometimes with very distressing conditions, which sometimes are humiliating for the patient and burdensome for the family. The relationship with the external world is compromised. Fear of loss of control over one's body and the social stigma of disability can be paralysing and can lead to intense feelings of isolation. Fear of disability and phantasies around it and around serious physical illness create an environment that is not conducive to patients feeling accepted or valued by the outside world. As a consequence, clients will sometimes declare a preference for a disabled counsellor from whom they will not feel so "different" and by whom they imagine they will be better understood.

Intrapsychic conflicts overlap with interpersonal affects: "Am I still an acceptable, loveable person", "Am I to blame for what has happened to me". Psychodynamic counselling is an opportunity to explore the unconscious and conscious meaning of the illness as it affects the client's identity.

Clients often have to deal with the loss of status in the world of work, which then highlights existing psychological problems that had been defended against:

A young man had developed an unusual form of epilepsy as a result of viral encephalitis; he was put on medication which prevented him from pursuing his career. His identity was totally dependent on his job; he had sought refuge in his profession and had no or very little personal life to fall back on. He had great difficulty in establishing trusting relationships. When he realized that the counselling was not going to restore his ability to work, he gradually stopped coming to his sessions. Some months later, however, he asked for a follow-up session and announced that he had joined a support group and was thinking of training as a therapist.

Clients have to deal with issues of trust and dependency. Relationships with relatives and partners are reassessed, and some are found wanting:

A young woman who was diagnosed with a degenerative and potentially disabling disease had not separated emotionally from home, even though she did not live in the same country as her parents. Her relationship with her parents had always been ambivalently dependent. Her father was a medical doctor and was seen by her, up to the time that she was diagnosed with the illness, as totally dependable and strong; however, (a) he had not protected her from the illness and (b) he had broken down in tears when he heard of the diagnosis. My client was devastated because she felt let down by him. It is possible that she turned to counselling in an effort to find a replacement parental figure, who, this time, would be really dependable.

Acquiring a life-threatening physical illness or a disability affects body-image and self-perception ("The ego is first and foremost a bodily ego": Freud, 1923, p. 26). Attacks on the integrity of the body are felt as direct attacks on the self. For example, the following case highlights the difficulty of seeing oneself as a sexual being when one has lost trust in one's body:

A woman who is recovering from treatment for cervical cancer had been given the "all clear" and had been advised that it would be good for her to resume her sexual relationship with her partner. However, she found it impossible to approach him on that subject. Up until recently she had found little fault in the relationship. Now she finds herself increasingly irritated by him and is able to confront him with the issues that upset her. However, her need for his reassurance that she is still desirable is just too painful to tackle in a straightforward manner.

Transference and countertransference

Consideration is given in the transference to the appropriateness and timing of interpretations. Working with the physical reality of a serious illness and disability, these considerations take on a different aspect. The aim of the work is to help the client adjust to the bodily blow to the self and to find his or her own meaning for the illness. Transference interpretations, based on the counsellor's countertransference reaction to the client's material, are made towards that end; the illness and disability are not interpreted. The client is looking for a "container for the altered state of his internal world, and attempting to recreate a sense of continuity, the 'going-on-being' that Winnicott (1956) describes as essential for psychic development and stability" (O'Gorman, 2000, p. 68).

The work will sometimes provide a corrective emotional experience to people who have not adjusted to a disability, even when acquired at birth. Deficiencies in the early environment affect psychological health and coping mechanisms (Kohut, 1980). Clients present with not being able to cope with life's stresses and express depressive feelings. Although initially they appear adjusted to their condition, it soon becomes clear that anger, frustration, and resentment at the disability, and their experience of a hostile and uncomprehending outside world, get in the way of leading a fulfilling life.

The material presented often contains memories of being subjected to long and regular sessions of physiotherapy and to painful operations, deemed necessary for the correction of physical impairments. The emphasis on physical development is perceived as being at the expense of unmet emotional needs. Psychological development is affected by the early environment. "Good-enough mothering" (Winnicott, 1960, pp. 145–146) gives the child the tools to deal with life's frustrations. The lack of that experience is felt as a loss of an accepting and valuing mirroring object and creates a kind of deficiency state. Life's frustrations and struggles are experienced as added losses. By allowing the client to reach and affect her or him—that is, by "taking the transference" (Mitrani, 2001)—the counsellor will allow "unacceptable" feelings to be expressed and provide a safe and empathic container for those feelings.

James S. Grotstein in his Foreword to Neville Symington's book *Narcissism: A New Theory* (1993) points to another view. He writes:

> He [N. Symington] has come to understand the narcissistic subject, not only from the well-known Kleinian instinctual grandiosity/manic defence standpoint or from the trauma-deficit conceptions of Fairbairn, Winnicott, Balint, and Kohut, but also from the unique perspective of profound ontological insecurity. . . . The infant/child becomes narcissistically disordered by making an unconscious choice, either towards the *lifegiver* (its authenticity or spontaneity) or to its disavowal and the use of magical pretence in order to evade psychic reality and to avoid external reality. [p. ix]

It is the child's response to the trauma which determines whether or not he or she will develop a healthy-enough defence mechanism that enables him or her to cope with life's vicissitudes.

Freud (1920) introduced the idea of the life and death instincts as the fundamental principles that regulate the activity of the organism. For Freud, the instincts are innate, biological, and present at birth; however, as they have opposite aims, they conflict: the life instincts "seek to combine more and more living substances into ever greater unities, and the death instincts . . . oppose this effort and lead what is living back into an inorganic state" (Freud, 1933, p. 107). The client's inner conflict is played out in the transference relationship. If the pull towards life is strong, the client will respond to the counsellor's efforts to reach him or her. A realignment of feelings towards the illness, an ability to see it as a turning point, will help the client adjust to the change. If, however, ambivalence, aggression, sadism, and masochism—all expressions of the death instinct—are prevalent, the pull towards self-destruction can overwhelm the therapeutic work.

Disability has been seen historically as a manifestation of the "other"; the difference has been viewed and treated with suspicion and fear. This applies in particular to disability acquired in the womb or at birth. Counselling a disabled client puts us in touch with our own feelings of being different and, therefore, vulnerable. We may unconsciously see our own "unacceptable" or "bad" self—that is, impaired, unsightly, the parts of ourselves we defend against—split-off and reflected in our disabled clients. As a result, we may be tempted to treat them "with kid gloves", reinforcing the feeling that the disability/illness is indeed unbearable. We may adopt a patronizing attitude and overcompensate by making allowances for difficult behaviour or be too accommodating to unreasonable demands. Awareness of and bringing into the open similarities and differences between client and counsellor will help establish beneficial counselling techniques.

Seeing oneself as different is occasionally translated as feeling not good enough to be treated by a non-disabled counsellor. Claims that only another disabled person can understand are often expressed early in the process, sometimes at the assessment stage. Acknowledgement of that feeling and working through the negative aspect of the transference are essential for engagement in the process. More destructive and difficult to acknowledge is the envy of the client of what is perceived as the counsellor's "good" health. Envy is corrosive both to the client and to the counsellor and is hard to defend against. When a treatment alliance has been established, mitigating the feelings of persecution and envy, the full impact of the loss can be addressed.

Disabled counsellors encounter similar problems: competition between client and counsellor on whose symptoms or impairments are more disabling can get in the way of a working alliance, and so does over-identification with the client or an inability to distance oneself appropriately when the feelings expressed resonate with the counsellor.

People with a serious illness have to face their fears of deteriorating physical ability, dependency, abandonment, and—with a life-threatening condition—death. These issues have to be dealt with realistically, even though they may well evoke the counsellor's own fears and anxieties. One of the common fantasies about death is that by talking about it, somehow we will make it happen. Counsellors have to find a way to help their clients talk about their concerns and anxieties about their death—for example, what is going to happen to the children and other members of their family they will leave behind, and how can the time remaining be used so that some of the anxieties can be resolved.

Some clients will reveal their rage and despair at what has happened to them by expressing suicidal ideation, something counsellors may find very hard to hear and to deal with. This attack on the counselling process is an expression of thwarted expectations of the treatments offered. The client needs to be helped to look at the anger that underlies the threat of suicide. Sometimes the feelings of anger and despair are unbearable, cannot be mediated, and are destructive enough to lead to a suicide attempt.

Counsellors can unwittingly block the expression of difficult and painful feelings or may attempt to rationalize the situation and lessen the impact of the grieving. Feelings of helplessness and hopelessness in distressing situations can be unbearable, and the urge to reassure the client can be overwhelming. Bion's concept of the container/contained (1984) is relevant to understanding these countertransference feelings. Because the client is often unable to think about his or her unbearable feelings or tolerate having them, they are projected into the counsellor. The counsellor needs to act as a container by being open to receiving the projections, being able to process the unbearable feelings, and transforming them into feelings that can be thought about.

Having experienced the medical model, people who suffer from a serious condition will bring to counselling a variety of expectations, some unrealistic. For example, there may be an unspoken hope that the talking therapy will be a cure, or will lead to a remission, or at least will alleviate the symptoms.

One of the defences often used to protect oneself from reality is splitting; the client may feel as if the medical profession has failed him or her, and the counsellor may be the subject of what Kohut (1971) terms an idealizing transference. The client will project onto the counsellor a sense of his or her own omnipotence; the counsellor will then be experienced as all powerful. Sandler, Dare, and Holder (1973) see the idealization of the therapist as "an idealisation that can defensively disguise and deny unconscious hostile feelings. Idealisation may break down (often quite dramatically) if the patient feels disappointed or if the underlying hostility becomes too strong" (p. 29). The counsellor needs to stay neutral and resist the temptation to be pulled into an unhelpful triangle. Frustrated by the counsellor not assisting in the way the client had

hoped, he or she can experience the counsellor as the "rejecting object" (Fairbairn, 1944, p. 114). From an object-relations perspective,
the rejecting object is a split-off aspect of the bad object, repressed
in the unconscious.

Disillusionment and/or strong hostility underlie the development of a negative transference. A way of thinking about the negative transference is Freud's structural model of the mind. Freud
states: "Since the transference reproduces the patient's relation
with his parents, it takes over the ambivalence of that relationship
as well. It almost inevitably happens that one day his positive attitude towards the analyst changes over into the negative, hostile
one. This, too, is usually a repetition of the past" (Freud, 1940
[1938], p 107).

Sandler, Dare, and Holder (1973) write: "(The) . . . transference
can be taken to include the unconscious (and often subtle) attempts
to manipulate or to provoke situations with others which are a
concealed repetition of earlier experiences and relationships, or the
externalisation of an internal object relationship" (p. 59).

The desire to be experienced as "good" counsellors may get
in the way of doing good psychodynamic work. Mitrani (2001)
writes: "If unbridled, it may prove to be the most obstructive 'desire' in Bion's sense of the word—since our patients may actually
need to transform us, in the safety of the transference relationship,
into the 'bad' object that does harm." Working through the negative transference is essential for the containment of unbearable
experiences. Mitrani (2001) goes on to write: "Most importantly,
that same object may also be experienced by the patient as able
to bear being 'bad' which in itself is 'good'. Furthermore, when
reintrojected by the patient in this modified form, the 'bad' object
is not so 'bad' at all; it is human, ordinary, with all the ordinary
human frailties imaginable, but it is bearable" (p. 1085).

* * *

Our physically ill and disabled clients need us to "survive" the
experience of hearing their distress and their anger. We need not to
give in to the temptation to treat them as "special" clients and therefore different from the rest and from us. Effective psychodynamic
work is characterized by acceptance and challenge, transference

interpretations and the monitoring of the countertransference, respecting essential defences, and attempting to overcome resistance. The resistance could be the result of the conflict between the innate drives, as Freud suggests; or environmental failure in the early mother–infant relationship, as Winnicott, Fairbairn, and Kohut suggest; or "ontological insecurity", as Symington suggests. Working with dual realities is not different in method; it is mainly about grieving for and overcoming loss. However, there will be some differences in the formulating and timing of interpretations and in the assessing of the degree of flexibility required to accommodate the physical reality that our clients experience.

CHAPTER EIGHT

What did you say?
What did you mean?

Michael Kelly

Therapy, in popular parlance, is often described as the "talking cure". Yet in a sense this presupposes that both client and counsellor can physically hear each other. When this most basic ingredient is missing, how can meaningful communication take place? In this chapter, I would like to present how, through counselling a deaf client, meaningful communication did take place that allowed for purposeful changes in the client's life. The client's name is Valerie.

Let's be honest—few of us give much time or thought to our senses. We use them automatically; they broaden and enhance our world and our experience of it. If we take a moment, we can imagine how the absence of one or more of our senses would limit us. Fitzgerald and Murray Parkes (1998) underline the importance of these functions when they write that

> sensory and cognitive functions enable us to orient ourselves in the world, they make us aware of dangers and rewards, they mediate many sources of pleasure and pain, and they are the means by which we receive messages from others. It follows that anything which seriously impairs sensory or cognitive function is bound to have psychological effects. [p. 57]

Throughout her life Valerie lived with the psychological effects of being deaf. It shaped her world, her behaviour, and how she engaged with it. It left deep psychological scars that only received attention when she was referred for counselling following the death of her boyfriend.

Fear can often dominate the life of a deaf person—fear of making mistakes, being misunderstood, avoided, ridiculed. New situations carry with them anxiety—anxiety about how the person will be perceived and accepted (Fitzgerald & Murray Parkes, 1998). Jack Ashley, a Member of Parliament for many years, described his deafness as "a lifelong burden" (Ashley, 1985). In this, Valerie was no different: "I hate being deaf, I am ashamed of my deafness and of my hearing aids," she told me in one session.

Valerie's history

Valerie was referred for counselling by a bereavement counsellor. She was an only child and is now in her late sixties, living alone, with a grown-up daughter and one grandson to whom she feels close. She worked all her life, retiring early fifteen years ago. Her parents separated and later divorced, after her mother had an affair during the war, when Valerie was 12, and this event marked her for life. Both parents remarried. Valerie spent the school year with her father and stepmother and the holidays with her mother and stepfather. She had a strained relationship with both her step-parents. Ironically, it was her stepfather who first discovered that she was deaf. She never realized her educational potential as she could only hear bits of what the teacher said and had to guess the rest. Failure to recognize her impaired hearing impacted upon the ways others responded to Valerie. She felt that she was perceived as, in her words, "an idiot", "an imbecile", and "stupid". She described a home life in which there was no discipline and where she could do what she liked. If we consider the contribution of our senses to the lifelong process of registering the boundary and link between self and other, we might wonder what it means to lack the function of hearing with a relatively unboundaried social environment, one in which we do not feel attended to. What are the implications for the task of self-definition and relatedness to others?

Valerie was offered a time-limited contract of eighteen months. She could not use sign language and therefore could not be assigned to one of the organization's team of dedicated counsellors who were deaf and who counselled through sign language. She learnt to lip-read, and this is how she was able to understand me.

"Acoustic problem"

Valerie's deafness—or "acoustic problem", as she almost always referred to it—had a huge impact on her. She never heard the sounds of the world. Not only could she not hear, but it also seems she did not have the language to say to anyone, "I cannot hear you".

As no one realized she was deaf, Valerie was left to put her own construction on what she saw. When others attempted to communicate with her, she could not hear them. All she could do was imagine what was being said. This led to misunderstanding and to her perception that people treated her badly. Internally she developed a persecutory outlook, a mindset in which her expectation was that she would be treated badly. This inner worldview was expressed in her frequently asked question: "Why do they do that? Why do they treat me like that? That is what I want to know."

Even when her deafness was diagnosed and some effort made at treatment, the stigma remained. Some showed compassion, while others continued to treat her as "an idiot". To many in the family she was an embarrassment. She felt excluded from family events. Valerie recalled two moments that were particularly painful. When an aunt died, her uncle was insistent Valerie should not attend the funeral as she would become "too emotional". For the same reason, she was not allowed to attend her own father's funeral.

Valerie's life has been dominated by feelings of loss and disappointment. Yet she could also be described as a survivor. She had the strength of character to face the many difficulties that life presented her with—being a single mother, holding down a full-time job, coping with her disability. I believe that this strength of character ultimately led her to counselling and enabled her to begin the process of facing the emotional trauma of her disability and its profound impact on her life.

The family

A theme that ran through every session and which was central to our work was Valerie's relationship with her family, both immediate, parental, and extended. They were spoken about with passion and presence. Each week they were introduced to me, and the kind of relationship she had with each one was carefully outlined. The family populated the room. They were real inside her; by speaking about them, she was, in a sense, letting them out.

They were divided into two distinct camps: those to whom she had a positive allegiance—that is, those who were supportive and helpful in a variety of ways—and those she experienced as behaving negatively towards her, labelling her, in her words, as "an idiot" and "stupid". Certainly they helped form her worldview, and the attitude of the second group predominated. They affected how she saw the world, experienced it, and how she expected to be treated by it.

In relating her experience of family week after week, she always spoke in the present tense, as if they were all still alive. Yet her parents and most of that generation of the family had been dead for many years. However, in her inner world they were very much present and alive. They gave her vitality and life; they lived on and were experienced again and again in the everyday interactions with others. They helped construct her expectation that in any relationship or interaction with another, she would be treated not with understanding and compassion but with ridicule and rejection. They became her persecutory inner objects. Each relationship provoked sensitivity as she watched for the slightest indication of how she was perceived. "I am very sensitive to how people respond to me," she told me in one session. Each interaction was examined minutely to discover how others were reacting to her and to confirm the family view, which she had introjected, that she was "an idiot" and "an imbecile". This dynamic showed itself in the most apparently innocent interactions, as with the pharmacist who misunderstood what she asked for and was roundly condemned for treating her like an idiot. "I told him I would take my business elsewhere," she remarked acidly.

I was the recipient of Valerie's projections. Her expectation and assumption was that I would behave towards her as the family did. Very early in counselling, using the material she presented, I challenged her assumption. Valerie admitted that she expected me to behave as her family had, fearing that I would not understand her. This fuelled an early negative transference. I found, by challenging this assumption in the transference, that a positive transference began to emerge and dominate. This strengthened the therapeutic container, allowing for deeper exploration of the material presented.

Holiday breaks provided another moment where this expectation featured. Breaks always had overtones of people leaving her, which triggered her anger and was expressed through her "cheeky" behaviour. While at a conscious level Valerie accepted the breaks, insisting that it was important for me to rest, unconsciously it revived her assumption that I was dismissing her and confirmed her view that I saw her as an idiot unworthy of any time and effort. Breaks provided fertile ground where this assumption could again be challenged and the beginning of a new understanding formed.

A pivotal moment in Valerie's life was the separation and divorce of her parents when she was 12. She came back to it again and again, allowing its impact, the pain, and disappointment to find expression. In some ways, the divorce was a useful container, a concrete event where all her feelings towards her non-attentive parents could be focused. In many respects, with her parents' divorce Valerie's world shut down, and she lived within that world ever since. Her memory of that time was clear as she recalled the effect it had on her. She remembered being told what her grandfather had said when her parents divorced: "not one of you realizes the effect this is going to have on that child." While Valerie was, in some sense, aware of the effect it had on her, perhaps for the first time, she began to put words to the immense pain and sense of guilt she felt.

Parents and family were always spoken about in an animated way, with anger and rage the predominant emotions. It was John Bowlby (1963) who suggested that anger may mask a deep sense of loss and should be understood as a "cry of protest, a reflection of need, of love and longing" (Kavaler-Adler, 2003). The family were vilified, condemned for the perceived way they treated Valerie. This condemnation was repeated week after week. Its constant repetition highlighted its importance. I gained insight into its possible meaning when I read what Lendrum and Syme wrote: "the vilification gets stuck with repeated condemnations it may be to protect the griever from extreme feelings of pain related to the lost love" (Lendrum & Syme, 2004, p. 173). This insight permitted me to see what Valerie was protecting herself from—the lost love of parents and family. Then, in the transference, we could begin to reconnect her with the feelings that she had been cut off from for so long.

Behaviour

Valerie's way of behaving was fashioned, in large part, by her "acoustic problem". This found expression in her manner, her dress, and the way she acted in sessions. She favoured short dresses of varying colours. Her mannerisms were often exaggerated, and she was given to acting theatrically during some sessions. All of this reflected the lack of containment and boundaries in Valerie's life.

On the way to the room to begin one session, Valerie described another client in the waiting-room as a "grapefruit head". When I asked her about this remark, she told me it was her way of being "cheeky". This was a phrase and a mode of behaviour that was used frequently, but it resembled how an adolescent might behave. In many ways Valerie was an adolescent, psychologically. The pre-counselling assessment report described her as regressed, and certainly she was, as her dress, mannerisms, attitude, and behaviour reflected an adolescent rather than a woman in her late sixties.

Each session had an intensity about it. This was reflected not just in the material presented, but in the way it was presented. Valerie used words but often acted out the events she was trying to convey. The room became her stage, and the acting out underlined the importance of what she was attempting to communicate. During one session she mimicked how other people walked, making them look idiotic. She was dismissive of them and their walk. The tissue box was another vehicle she used, often to express her anger. It was turned upside down, put on the floor, sometimes banged violently on the table. Observing this "play", she was inviting me to see and hear and respond to her vivid communication.

The interpretation I would offer would often be responded to by Valerie with the phrase: "that is what I was thinking and you have confirmed it for me" or "you are confirming it. I know what I was thinking was right."

Valerie realized that to achieve any form of change she would have to face the pain of how she had experienced being treated by parents, family, and others. Towards the end of one particularly intense and somewhat chaotic session, I commented on the level of pain she was expressing. She was silent for a moment then said: "I will have to face the hurt and pain. I know I have to do that."

Her life was peppered with losses. Her way of defending against the powerful emotions these losses provoked was to behave "cheekily", act like an adolescent, and often laugh inappropriately, which hid the sadness she felt. The principal loss was the loss of hearing. It disabled her, left her vulnerable and at the mercy of others. She gave me an example of how vulnerable she felt when during one session she used the phrase, "the wedding that never was". I asked her what she meant by this. She told me that in her thirties she was in a relationship with a man by whom she became pregnant. They decided to marry. The day of the wedding arrived, and Valerie and all the invited guests were at the register office. He never turned up. Valerie said: "the cake was there, the guests were there and all the presents. The people were very nice and allowed me to keep the presents." I noted that her mode of expression was quite childish, such that it almost removed all feeling from this painful and embarrassing incident. Yet I felt a profound sense of loss and pain. I commented on this sense of sadness. Valerie replied that she agreed it was sad but that now she was letting it go, and she gestured with her arms that something was flowing from her. I was helping her to let it go, she told me. Up to that moment in the session, I felt I was in the presence of an adolescent. Her mannerisms, expression, and repetition of words or phrases reminded me of a child. In the way she responded to me, acknowledging the sadness and loss, I connected momentarily with the adult Valerie.

Towards the end of that session, she told me that the only people who understood her were Londoners and Irish people. She described them as sympathetic and compassionate. I felt that this was her way of telling me I had heard her and that her pain and loss were understood.

Her behaviour, mannerisms, and acting out in sessions could also be understood as a form of evacuation—her way of letting go, as suggested in the previous paragraph. The containment I offered allowed us to give meaning to the feelings. They were painful but also meaningful, and this meaning is the beginning of the making of a self.

Valerie used images of contemporary life as reference points to her past. Hence, the way people treated her always reminded her of her experience of childhood. These moments from everyday life provoked a response—sometimes anger but, more often than not, "cheeky" behaviour. Once she spoke about the crowds of people she had encountered on her way to the session. The bus was full, the pavements packed. Valerie felt ignored and lost as she made her way through the crowds. "They remind me of my family", she said becoming more animated. She then used an expletive, repeated it several times, and laughed out loud, adding "I love saying that". This was followed by a two-fingered salute directed at a number of empty chairs stacked against the wall. It was as if those members of her family whom she hated were occupying the chairs. I felt she was testing me to see what she could get away with or to see if I would behave like her aunts and disapprove of her.

Jung in his writings underlined the importance of telling one's story in the presence of another who can comment on it. The weekly counselling sessions became the place where Valerie could tell her story for the first time and have it listened to and understood. Throughout her life, Valerie's deafness had inhibited her comprehension of the world and left her to fill in the gaps, developing a mode of behaviour without reference to anything outside herself. The weekly session, during which Valerie expressed herself, through speech and action, allowed some of those gaps to be closed, bringing meaning and a developing sense of self.

Valerie often described her behaviour as "cheeky" and at times revelled in behaving in this way. This was that part of her, the playful child, that was finding expression. Counselling sessions became the place where the "cheeky" child could "play" through words, gesture, laughter, and sometimes tears. Her "cheeky" behaviour conveyed many messages and had many meanings. The behaviour was sometimes used as a defence against the sadness she felt. It acted as a signpost to the pain of being ignored and dismissed as "an idiot". More often than not, her behaviour was used with the intention of making others notice and respond to her. I recall that during one session Valerie quite suddenly threw her feet on the table. The gesture was somewhat dramatic and adolescent in nature, but it was used to communicate something to me. What was at issue were Valerie's feelings about being ignored, not cared for or supported. This was what she was telling me, and I was not hearing it. By focusing on the meaning of her gesture, I could "see" what she was trying to communicate. Through the counselling process these communications were heard, spoken about, and reflected on, leading to a new and different understanding. Valerie described this as "very valuable and worth thousands".

Towards an ending

Interwoven through all our sessions was the theme of loss and ending. The approaching end of counselling brought these issues into sharper focus. Now it was our ending we were facing. We were approaching the end of a therapeutic relationship that had affected both of us. Valerie's way of expressing her feelings about our ending would follow the pattern and practice of previous separations (Coren, 2001). Acting out, behaving "cheekily", and the material she would bring to sessions would all point to how she was feeling about our ending. Her pattern was to project her feelings into other events and people. It was important in our final sessions that these projections be taken back and placed where they belonged, in the room.

A frequent and familiar theme raised at this time was Valerie's perception of not being cared for. Many examples were cited to back up her assumption. I said to her that just as she felt not cared for by others, she also, in her mind, felt not cared for by me because I was bringing counselling to an end. Valerie found it difficult to accept the link, and she could only respond by saying, "I shall miss coming here".

Often the pain of ending and separation from me was expressed through her anger, which found its outlet in her "cheeky" behaviour. During one of the final sessions when she was particularly angry, she put her feet on the table once again. It was a provocative act. She looked at me to see how I would respond. I was so taken aback by the suddenness of the movement that I could not help but laugh. Valerie said, "You are laughing at me for putting my feet on the table. You want me to sit prim and proper." She then mimicked sitting in a prim and proper manner. She then laughed out loud. I responded by drawing together what she said and did and how I reacted, focusing on its meaning: the pain of our separation. Valerie laughed again—inappropriately, I felt—but I knew the laughter was her way of expressing the sadness she felt.

As our ending approached, Valerie produced a notebook. Each week she noted the points she wished to talk about. As each point was attended to, it was ticked off or crossed out. Once all the points on the page were dealt with, the page was torn out, crunched up into a ball, and thrown into a nearby wastepaper basket. This was important, as it signified Valerie letting go of what had bound her, ushering in what she described as "a sense of freedom".

Valerie expressed how painful our separation was in many ways. The dress she wore to our final sessions was always black, a colour often associated with death and mourning. That is what our ending felt like to her, a death. I also understood it as an invitation to put words on the unbearable pain of our ending, which Valerie expressed in this rather poignant way: "the people who are kind to me are now dead." On other occasions she would open a session by enquiring how many sessions were left. This provided another opportunity to focus on how painful our ending was.

In a sense, our ending brought us right back to her beginnings and to her primary attachment figure. All subsequent relationships were based on this earliest relationship. This relationship and the experiences that followed through childhood developed a set of expectations and assumptions that allowed her to view the world and engage with it in a particular way. Through the counselling experience, but particularly as the ending approached, these expectations and assumptions were addressed, and challenged in the transference, permitting some changes to take place. She told me at the end of our penultimate session: "I have made many changes since coming to see you. People notice it. People are treating me differently."

In the final session, I asked Valerie what this experience had meant to her. She said: "What you have given me is my freedom. I feel free now. That is what you have given me, and that is what I will be taking away from here."

Conclusion

I found it significant that Valerie wished to talk about her late "boyfriend" in the last session. In a way, the issues it raised—loss and ending—had been the predominant themes of our work together.

Valerie struggled with an "acoustic problem", as she described it, all her life. Her impaired hearing had had profound consequences for her. Her education had suffered as she was unable to hear all the teacher said. What she could not hear she guessed. This developed a mindset that she carried throughout her life. This, together with a rather persecutory view of the world, led to feelings of being stigmatized, feeling an outsider, rejected, belittled, and—her favourite phrase—"being treated like an idiot". In the process she rejected herself and replaced it with a survival persona. She was sensitive in all relationships, as her expectation was that she would be rejected. This played itself out in the counselling relationship, as she anticipated that I would adopt the same posture. I feel that one of the reasons counselling was beneficial for her was the fact that I did not.

A significant loss for her was the separation and divorce of her parents when she was 12. She could not accept this and felt negatively about her new stepmother and stepfather. Both came to symbolize the negative bad side of her. Her desire was to rejoin the parental couple, and much of our work was dealing with the disappointment that this would never happen. While at a more conscious level I feel she accepted this, at a deeper level I felt she still holds out the hope that it might.

The divorce of her parents created another mindset in terms of her behaviour. To many it seemed childish, and in many respects it was. Focusing on her behaviour allowed us to explore the pain and loss of the parental couple and the other losses in her life. The anger she felt then, and which manifests itself now in the events of everyday life, is expressed not simply in a verbal way but primarily by acting "cheekily". This mindset is ingrained, and, while exploration has helped make it more present, it has been hard for her to change it significantly.

Towards the end she produced a notebook containing her thoughts and feelings and incidents she wished to focus on. I thought it significant that, as each page was dealt with, it was torn out and consigned to the dustbin, as if symbolically letting go of the feelings and thoughts attached to that particular issue.

While there was an initial negative transference, a positive transference dominated. It was difficult for Valerie to acknowledge ambivalent feelings. Towards the end, however, she could acknowledge some of the help her stepfather gave her, suggesting that she could see both the "good" and "bad" sides of him, a moment's recognition of the two sides of her.

The experience of counselling was positive for Valerie. The ending was painful yet was faced, and the pain and loss were acknowledged. The experience has, in some ways, allowed her to lay to rest some of the ghosts of the past.

CHAPTER NINE

Becoming free

Anne Green

In about 1986 it was suggested to me by the disability team that maybe it would help to go and see a counsellor. Not because I wasn't coping with life, but because I had a lot to cope with. For example, I have cerebral palsy, and in 1978 I had developed ongoing problems with my voice, which is quiet at best of times but can disappear altogether. However, I never knew from one day to the next how it would be and, if I were having a bad patch, how long it would last for. In 1979 I had developed problems with my bladder, and in 1983 it became difficult for me to swallow. By 1986, quite suddenly, I was unable to swallow liquids at all. The liquid would sit in the front of my mouth and, when I attempted to swallow, most of the liquid would explode out of my mouth. I soon became dehydrated and had to find another way to obtain nourishment. This is why I was given a permanent gastrostomy, which is a feeding tube that is inserted directly into the stomach, by a surgical procedure. I was aware that I was receiving the best possible medical treatment and support that I could regarding my physical problems. However, I needed a lot of emotional support and reassurance. The medical profession dealing with me did not have the expertise and time to give me the additional emotional support I needed. Therefore they suggested gently that maybe I needed to go and see a counsellor.

* * *

The thought of going for counselling made me feel that I wasn't coping with life, that I was a failure and a nuisance to everyone. I was ashamed to admit this, and because of this I debated for over a year whether or not I should accept counselling. After a lot of unnecessary torment, I decided to look into it. Because of my voice problems, one of the people trying to persuade me to go agreed, with my permission, to ring the Westminster Pastoral Foundation on my behalf and make an appointment for me. It turned out that before I was offered an appointment, I had to fill in a form that was very personal, but allowed me to be very honest about why I felt I needed counselling. I knew I had to be absolutely honest or it would be a waste of time. This made me think of what I didn't like about myself, which is a very negative way of interpreting my problems. I can say this now, but I couldn't then. Let me give an example: If people did not react the way I expected them to, I would think they were cross with me. I knew, deep down, that at the age of 42 it was a bit immature to be always saying "are you cross with me?" or "do you mind?" They both meant the same thing. Obviously, perhaps once in fifty times someone would be cross. If I made a phone call and someone was sharp with me—probably because they were busy with other things—I would think the end of the world had come. I would want to ring back and say I was sorry. If they were busy it would aggravate the situation even more, and often they were embarrassed and did not know what to say. This mainly happened with people who were working with me, or people I was fond of and had a deeper relationship with. Deep down I knew I wanted to overcome this, but I did not know how to. So on that form I dared to say that I wanted help to overcome this problem.

That is not to say that I didn't want to talk about problems relating to disabilities or relationships, but basically I knew I wanted to change inside me but did not know how to go about it. So I tried to put this on the form. About a week later I had a letter giving me an appointment and telling me that, if it was easier, I could fill the form in when I got there. The initial appointment did not mean that you had been accepted or were eligible for counselling help; the interview was to decide the kind of help that was needed.

* * *

I remember it was the 12th of May, 1988. I went to WPF in Kensington, and a lady with fair hair, wearing a green anorak, met me, and I thought I would never be able to open up to her. We walked across the tennis courts into the centre specifically for disabled people. I had already told her that I needed a chair with good head support. She explained that they hadn't got the right chair today, but they would order it. Then the interview began. It took a bit of time for her to get tuned in to the way I talk, but she was very patient and calm. What I remember the most about the interview was that she did not have the form in front of her. But she was able to remember most of what I had said on it. My first interview lasted for one and a half hours. I can remember a mixture of feelings: someone was listening to me, I felt drained after pouring out all sorts of problems, I felt yes, maybe I could talk to this lady, after all, but not every week. I decided I liked her by the end of the interview, but I wanted to run away where no one could see me. What we had talked about had been very deep and intense. I remember feeling tired, but I had another meeting to go to. On reflection, if I had remembered earlier, I could have put it off and gone home to bed.

When I did get home, I cried. At last the ice had been broken. My next appointment was a week on Tuesday. At that time I only paid £3 an hour, but as costs went up, the fee increased, until I was paying £10 per session, which proves that they are not in it for the money.

After going for counselling for a few weeks, I began to realize it was helping me to talk about my feelings. I realized it was a safe place where I could say what I liked and not be judged. On the other hand, I felt very guilty going to someone once a week just to talk about me. I tried for about six months to convince Ruth that I only needed to come once a fortnight. Finally, on one occasion Ruth said to me "alright, make it once a fortnight", and then she booked a date for me to come two weeks later. I cannot remember what was in my mind at the time, but when it got nearer to the day I originally should have been going, I felt that I really wanted to go.

It so happened that I was in the area, so I dared to go over to the centre and ask if Ruth was around. She met me in the corridor and said we should go to her room. I can't remember my exact words, but I said something like, "Are you free tomorrow?" She smiled and said, "Yes, is there something you would like to talk about?" I just said yes and didn't know where to look, as I knew what Ruth must be thinking; perhaps, also, I felt embarrassed. Ruth was not judgemental, but with a smile and a twinkle in her eye she said: "I don't know what we are going to do with you. See you on Wednesday." I remember then that all I wanted to do was get away from the building. When we did meet, I think Ruth said that we should meet once a week from now on. What could I do, but agree with her? But there was no need for me to feel embarrassed: Ruth had worked with many people in similar situations.

Looking back, my wish to go and see her once a fortnight was unrealistic, as I was beginning to understand some of my negative feelings. I was starting to realize that I could overcome them. Unfortunately, I wanted to be able to do it all in one go. Ruth warned me that it would be a long process, but that I would improve. Then something quite unconnected would happen—for instance, I would have to go into hospital for an operation and would therefore be put in a vulnerable position once more. This would make me feel more insecure. It was hard for me to accept the reality, but, in fact, after many years of having to cope with my negative feelings, I began to be able to control them. I recognized them for what they were, and I could see them in the right context. On one occasion I walked into the session and said "Guess what—I've done it again!" If I remember, I had asked someone if they were cross with me, and as soon as I had said it I realized that I had got the wrong end of the stick. I was able to talk about it and see it in a different light—after all, this was what I had told Ruth I wanted to overcome.

* * *

Once I had settled down to going for counselling, I wanted to make the best of the opportunity I had been given, and I normally made a list of what I wanted to talk about. On one or two occasions I did think it would have been easier for me to sit at my computer and type out what I wanted to say and give it to Ruth, but she discouraged me because the whole point of the sessions was to get in touch with my feelings by talking about them. The reason Ruth wasn't keen on my idea was that if I had written down what I wanted to say, I wouldn't have been in the position to be spontaneous. I can appreciate this now, but I did not at the time. Sometimes it was not possible to get through everything I wanted to in one hour. This was partly my own fault, because I needed to get the trivial things out of the way first. I had a habit of coming out with something quite important, when there was only about two minutes of my session left to go! Ruth used to say, "We will have to look at why, with two minutes to go, you come out with something really important, when we don't have time to talk about it." Obviously I did not do this on a conscious level. On reflection, I wonder if it was only just before the time ran out that I could pluck up the courage to say what was on my mind. In time, I did improve. Actually I think it is quite a common problem with people who have started having counselling.

* * *

As I mentioned earlier, I have a feeding tube, and I found this very difficult to come to terms with. I remember one day we were sitting talking about it, and Ruth was very supportive and gentle. I remember feeling very drained and left her room almost in tears. She suggested I sit in the garden until I was ready to leave. I later found out that by the time I got to the door she knew I was in tears. My time was up, and the unspoken rule was that you contain your feelings until the next time you met. I can remember sitting on a bench and wondering if Ruth would come near me as she walked across to the other department. Perhaps I just wanted to get away from it all. If I remember rightly, I came home and went to bed for an hour. That was the beginning of the healing process, and when I returned the next week we talked about it again, only this time I was much more composed. However, this was far from the last time I shed tears. Looking back, this was a growing point.

* * *

As a practising Roman Catholic, my swallowing disability affected the way I received Communion. In my church we always receive Communion in the form of a wafer (the Host), but it can also be given in the form of wine. I was very upset because, to begin with, I didn't know this and I would struggle with the Host, which would get caught in my mouth. My parish priest arranged for me to see the bishop, whom I knew, and he asked me to tell him how he should tell the priests which was the best way to give me Communion. I explained that I wanted a little drop of the wine put on a spoon and given to me. It was very hard for the priests to realize why I could not take a small particle of the host. I found this very upsetting, because I felt it was a barrier to my integrating into the church community, although I knew that in receiving the wine or the Host I was receiving Communion. I did discuss this with close friends from the church, and Ruth encouraged me to talk about it when it was on my mind.

* * *

Since the early 1970s I have had problems with my neck, with referred pain going down my arms. When the pain is bad, it makes me feel more disabled and causes me to cry. Sometimes when I am sitting in my armchair, I need to support my arms. Ruth always tried to make sure that there was a cushion there for me. However, when the pain was bad, I could not attend a session. This was very frustrating. The medical professionals think that the pain is caused by the nerves pressing on the muscles. This is probably due to the way I move my head and the way I walk. Sometimes I would talk to Ruth about the pain and the effect it had on me.

* * *

One of the good things about going to a counsellor is that I did not only talk about the problems relating to my disability. It also gave me the opportunity to talk about relationships and women's problems. For eighteen years of my life I was running a club for disabled and able-bodied children. In 1992 I had to give the club up, for health considerations. This broke my heart for a number of reasons: I had formed the club, it had been a part of my life for eighteen years, and many disabled and able-bodied children had gone through my hands. After retiring from the club, it really hit me how much I loved children and how much I missed not having a child of my own to care for. I could not believe how intense I found the pain to be. Ruth gave me the opportunity to work through these feelings and helped me to realize that mine was a normal, healthy reaction. However, this was something I would have to come to terms with. Again, it was not something that would be cleared up in one or two sessions—in fact, the problems did keep showing themselves in different ways for about five years. At least I was able to work through the feelings. Now if they surface, I know how to deal with them. More importantly, I realized that they are perfectly normal feelings, and had I not had the opportunity to talk about them in depth, they could have caused me to become very bitter—who knows? By this time we were meeting every two weeks, as I was managing so much better.

* * *

I had a brother called Joseph, who was born with "water on the brain" (the medical name is hydrocephalus). Joseph and I were very close—most brothers and sisters have some kind of bond, but Joseph was a very special person in my life. We played and went on holiday together. At the age of 14, he developed meningitis and ended up in a mental hospital. I used to try to go and see him every month, whether he knew me or not. My other brothers and sisters had grown up with him until he was 11, and although they knew his problems, he was just part of our family. However, they found it hard to visit him in hospital, because they wanted to remember him as he was, not like a baby in the womb that he seemed to be, at times, when I saw him. Although Joseph died in 1983, my memories of him lingered on for many years, and this was another issue I was able to discuss freely with Ruth. In one sense, this helped me to understand my parents' pain more deeply. Because I was disabled and had a disabled brother, I could see the picture from both sides of the coin. When my father died, I was asked by the family to say a bidding prayer, with words to the effect that Dad would now be with his son. I can remember this having a great impact on me.

* * *

My father had cancer in 1996, diagnosed in the November, and he died in the May of the following year, having been given six months to live. After he died, I went back to having counselling once weekly, for about six months, to help me cope with grieving for my father's death. For me it was very helpful, as I always felt that Dad had mixed feelings about me being disabled, but in fact he was very proud of me. Being able to talk about some of these issues helped me not only with grieving, but also to appreciate that Dad was a very good father and to see him in a better light.

My brothers and sisters are very fond of and, I think, proud of me. But because I grew up away from home, it was difficult for them to realize all I was able to do and to treat me as an equal. I found this painful in the past but have adjusted to it now. They have their own families and lifestyles, and I have had to accept this as part of life; in time the pain or disappointment was put into perspective, but I needed help to do this.

Another problem I encountered to do with my disability was when my mother became ill and disabled and for a time needed care in hospital. My father had to cope on his own; my brothers and sisters visited and helped my mother when they could, but as they lived far away and are all married, this was not frequently. I found it painful and difficult that even though I was single and the oldest daughter, I was not able to go and look after her the way I wanted to. I know what it feels like to be disabled, so I knew how my mother felt when she was incapacitated.

* * *

In 1999, Ruth changed her job, and she asked me what I felt I wanted to do about seeing her. I was very touched when she actually offered to let me go and see her in her own home, but I wanted time to think about it. On reflection, it would have been a great pity to lose that contact, as although I did not feel that I needed to see Ruth on a regular basis, it gave me confidence to know that if something did crop up, I had someone I could turn to. I think it is important to mention that it might not be something dramatic: I remember I got very overtired once and was overreacting to silly little things and unconsciously making mountains out of molehills. Just being able to talk about it without being judged gave me the opportunity to put things into perspective and confirmed that I was coping.

Some years have passed by now, but I can still recall and use what I learnt in our counselling sessions.

CHAPTER TEN

A life well lived:
the challenge of progressive disability

Ruth Archer

From time to time a disabled person was referred to the service, and when the disability included speech or hearing problems, care had to be taken to ensure that communication would be possible between client and therapist. Other details that required attention were, in some instances, transport problems, parking facilities, and accommodation for wheelchairs. These arrangements were necessary to ensure that the client was able to attend sessions regularly, but they would affect the therapeutic relationship and stimulate a variety of countertransference feelings.

Psychodynamic work with disabled people requires the therapist to have an understanding of both the individual disability and the way in which the condition affects the person with whom they are working. Without this understanding the work will be hampered, and, although it may take some time for an able-bodied person to understand the many aspects of a person's disability, that understanding can probably never be total.

* * *

Anne, who was in her early forties, was referred to WPF by the Disability Team at her local hospital in May 1988. She was unable to fill out our pre-assessment questionnaire, or make the initial phone call, but these difficulties were overcome with the help of a friend. The reality of her need to depend on others was therefore apparent from the first contact.

Normally the assessment interview would be carried out by a counsellor who would not have continued with the ongoing work, but in this instance it was felt that this would not be helpful, and, as I had a vacancy, it was agreed that I would meet with Anne to explore whether we could work together.

Anne had cerebral palsy, a condition of which I had some knowledge. Nevertheless, I was still unprepared for the range of her disabilities. Anne was able to walk, but she had a lurching gait and on occasion had been accused of being drunk. The main problem as far as our sessions were concerned was her voice. Anne had a speech impediment, and her disability affected her vocal chords, so that at times she could not raise her voice above a whisper. To do so caused her pain in her jaw and also her diaphragm. At WPF we use chairs, and we had to place them closer together than usual in order for me to hear what she said. I had to tune in to her voice and speech. At the beginning, if I could not understand something that Anne said, I said so and she would repeat it. I decided to do this rather than guess from the context what she was trying to say. This slowed the process down and tried the patience of both of us, but we persevered and eventually achieved a good-enough level of communication. It was also necessary to obtain a special chair for Anne that would support her head while she was sitting, and this enabled her to be reasonably comfortable during the sessions. She wore a neck support to align her spine while walking, but usually removed this when she arrived, as it restricted her head movements.

Anne developed cerebral palsy at birth following a difficult breech delivery. She was the second eldest of eight children, one of whom, Joseph, died at the age of 33 years when Anne was 36 years old. This brother suffered from hydrocephalus and developed learning difficulties, but Anne and he were very close. Joseph was initially able to attend a mainstream school, but later went to a boarding-school for disabled children. When a second disabled child was born, Anne's parents found it difficult to cope with their growing family of five children, two of whom required special attention. At the age of 4 years, Anne was admitted to an orthopae-dic hospital in Middlesex. Her parents and siblings, particularly her mother, visited Anne every two weeks, but the separation was traumatic for Anne and made her feel that she was too difficult for anyone to cope with. This was to emerge in the transference many years later.

Anne remained at the hospital until she was 9 years old and able to walk unaided. She had been able to visit home a couple of times during those years, but she felt it was difficult to really get to know her brothers and sisters. Anne was transferred from the hospital to a Roman Catholic boarding-school for physically handicapped children, where she remained until she was 17. She was able to go home for the holidays, and when she left school she returned home to live. Later Anne went to college in Bristol to do her "O" and "A" levels, where she enjoyed the company of other young people and had her first experience of living in a hostel.

* * *

Congenital physical disability interferes with the normal progress from dependence to independence that the physically healthy child enjoys. Anne was physically dependent on others throughout her childhood and into her adult life, although she struggled to attain independence, and when I met her she was living alone in her own flat. However, she needed the help of several people in order to do this and was unable to spend twenty-four hours alone with-out assistance with basic bodily care. Although Anne employed her own carers, she needed the backup of social services and was frequently frustrated by the system breaking down. Striving for emotional independence from the people on whom she relied for physical care was a difficult area for Anne to negotiate. However, she was a dependent mature adult and not a dependent child, and this needed to be recognized.

The conflict between the need for a 40-year-old intelligent woman to control and run her own life and the inability of her body to grant her that freedom was always present.

This conflict emerged as we negotiated the contract. Anne wanted to come fortnightly rather than weekly, but with obvious reluctance she agreed to weekly sessions. When we discussed this, she said she did not want to become dependent. We met weekly for about eight weeks, with Anne insisting each week that she preferred fortnightly sessions. It had become an unhelpful battle of wills, and with some reluctance I agreed to fortnightly sessions for a trial period. I think that at the time I felt that she needed some autonomy. I was also concerned that she might end the therapy prematurely. Her resistance appeared to be limited to the question of frequency, as she engaged well in the sessions and, although sometimes late, attended regularly.

The first gap week of the fortnightly sessions arrived, and the day before we would normally have met Anne arrived at the WPF and asked to see me. The following day the weekly sessions were reinstated at her request, and we were able to look at the whole issue of dependency more closely and in a much more meaningful way. It was the beginning of her working through this painful area of her life.

* * *

One of the reasons that Anne came into therapy was because she was losing her ability to swallow, something that she had always had difficulty with. In spite of all efforts to prevent this, the loss of the ability to eat and drink, to taste food, and to enjoy its texture was inevitable. Anne was naturally very distressed by this turn of events, and I experienced an overwhelming sense of helplessness, which was to some degree a projection of the helplessness that Anne felt but could not afford to acknowledge and, at the same time, maintain her ability to cope. I felt it was important to "hold" this for Anne until such time as she felt able to confront the enormity of what had happened to her. This was a gradual process and illustrated the necessity of not undermining a person's defences until she or he is ready to deal with the underlying pain.

Anne had previously had several operations on her bladder, and subsequently she had to have a catheter inserted into it permanently through her abdomen. It was not long before she also had a tube inserted through her abdomen into her stomach, through which she would be fed for the rest of her life. It took some time for Anne to adjust to this new arrangement, but she become adept at feeding herself and was even able to change the tube herself!

However, the loss of the basic function of eating, which we all take for granted, was devastating and brought into focus another loss, which was her lack of a sexual partner.

As a practising Roman Catholic by birth and belief, Anne had embraced celibacy as an offering to God, and she felt that it both enriched her life and gave it meaning. Anne had some good male friends, including one or two priests, who offered her support over a number of years, but she grieved for what she felt had been denied her, and it was important to acknowledge the significance of this loss. When she understood that she did not need to feel guilty about mourning the loss of a "normal" experience, it became easier to allow her feelings to surface.

Anne had long realized that she would not be able to have children (she had had a hysterectomy some years previously), and she also felt this loss acutely. For eighteen years Anne had run a club for disabled and able-bodied children over the summer. For various reasons she decided she would have to give this up, but the gap it left in her life accentuated the loss of children of her own. The pain of this realization, added to the other losses, was palpable. We worked with it over a number of years, returning to it when needed until some degree of acceptance was gained.

Anne was a free spirit trapped in a failing body, and she awoke each morning to the knowledge that physically nothing would change. Sometimes Anne felt depressed, which was not surprising, but I was impressed by her adaptation and the generosity she showed towards those who misunderstood her. However, Anne expressed very little anger, and in general she found it difficult to express negative feelings, particularly during the early stages of our therapeutic work. This difficulty was linked to her physical dependency needs, which were always present, and her fear that she was "too much" for people and might alienate them. If any of her carers or professional helpers were not available when she needed them, Anne felt she had been too demanding and would apologise. She feared people getting cross with her, as this would confirm her worst fears. The more significant the relationship, the more anxiety was created. It took some time for Anne to recognize that if her speech therapist, whom she had known for a number of years, was slightly abrupt on the telephone, it was because she was tired or busy and it was not necessarily Anne who had elicited that response. This situation was often repeated with other people whom Anne depended on or was close to.

Inevitably, this concern was apparent in our sessions also, and thus we were able to work with it. Anne was keen to overcome this difficulty, as she was aware of her inner child who became activated on these occasions. Having spent most of her childhood in hospitals, it was understandable that she felt insecure in her relationships. The usual developmental progress had been further hampered by her ongoing physical needs.

One of the frustrations we both encountered was the problem of her arriving on time for her sessions. Anne had to travel by taxi, which she booked in advance. Sometimes the taxi failed to turn up or was late, which meant that she too was late. Knowing that I would be waiting and might therefore "be cross" was a source of anxiety for Anne. My concern was that I was "short-changing" her, because to maintain the boundaries we always ended on time; in addition, her speech problems slowed things up. I therefore felt that she did not have as much therapeutic space as other people did and was thus being further disadvantaged. This caused me some discomfort, but as we were able to share our feelings about this situation impinging on our sessions, it became easier for us both to manage it.

Gradually, Anne became able to express her anger and frustration, without the fear that she would be abandoned by those on whom she was dependent. This emotional separation from her caregivers and friends gave her an emotional independence she had previously not experienced. Since she no longer needed to project her angry feelings on to others and fear their retaliation, she was able to relinquish her omnipotent defence, and in doing so she found a new freedom to be herself.

* * *

Within her physical limitations, Anne was an active member of her church and community. Her ability to use a computer meant that she could undertake course work, and this enabled her to enrol for a pastoral studies course at Heythrop College. When this was completed she began a social-science degree course with the Open University. Special arrangements had to be made for the examinations, as Anne had to dictate her answers to a designated person.

This was hard on her voice, which at the best of times caused her problems. Essays were less of a problem, and Anne worked hard at her studies. Anne had always been active on behalf of the disabled, but she was concerned that "she was contributing so little to society". The children's holiday club had given her a sense of purpose and fulfilment, which she lost when she had to give it up. In 1986 this had been recognized when she was awarded a medal for services to children. Later, Anne served on the local Health Committee, and she wrote two small books on disablement issues and a third, autobiographical work was published in 1996. No mean achievement, but, as she got older and her physical problems increased, Anne had to rely more on her intellectual gifts for fulfilment, and she struggled to accept her limitations.

* * *

One of the most difficult things for Anne to cope with was the fluctuations in her voice: one day it would be quite strong, the next she was unable to speak except in a whisper. Anne had a machine that could print out what she wanted to say on ribbon-sized paper, which because of its length was not all that easy to read. Later she acquired a battery-operated amplifier with a small microphone that was held in place by headphones. This was an improvement, but occasionally our sessions had to end early as Anne had pain in her jaw and diaphragm caused by the effort involved in trying to communicate.

Another problem that Anne had to contend with was severe neck pain. Physiotherapy helped but was not always available. The pain extended down her arms and sometimes made it hard for her to concentrate in the sessions. Eventually acupuncture afforded her some relief, but the pain was very persistent and debilitating.

During the time that I was working with Anne, she had four operations on her bladder, bringing the total number of operations to over twenty. In addition, the gastrostomy tube sometimes had to be re-sited, which also required surgery. Anne was away for quite some time following one of the operations, and I visited her in hospital once and followed this up with a home visit. It was important to maintain the continuity of our work, as extended breaks meant that Anne had less support during these periods of hospitalization. Both of Anne's parents were in poor health at the time, particularly her mother, and Anne was distressed that she was unable, as the eldest daughter, to support her parents as much as she would like to be able to. Anne's brothers and sisters were all married, some with families, and they tended to relate to her as their disabled sister, who had grown up away from them. Her hospitalizations, and the other treatments she needed, tended to confirm this view, and Anne made huge efforts to secure her place in the family, as a person who had a viewpoint and a contribution to make regardless of her disability.

* * *

As time went on, Anne's ability to swallow decreased, in spite of exercises and the efforts of her speech therapist to improve the response of the muscles of the swallowing reflex. Eating any food at all had become dangerous and life-threatening for Anne, as the food would enter her lungs and choke her, or cause her to have serious chest infections. Not to be able to have even a small cup of tea increased her sense of deprivation, as feeding via the gastrostomy tube by-passed the taste buds; although her hunger was satisfied, she missed out on one of the basic pleasure of life. I was impressed, therefore, by her attitude when she attended functions where food was served, as she encouraged other people to eat in her presence and sometimes invited friends for a meal at her home, even though she was unable to eat the food herself. It was difficult, however, for people to understand the severity of the problem or its permanence; this became particularly acute when Anne, as a practising Roman Catholic, wanted to take Communion, which in the Catholic church is in the form of a wafer (the Host), which Anne was unable to swallow. This setback was very distressing, and Anne was deeply upset because so many people failed to understand why she could not take just a small part of the Host. The struggle she had to participate in the Communion caused her even greater anguish and increased her isolation from the rest of the congregation, who participated in the Mass without problems. It was as if God Himself had rejected her, and although she knew that this was not the case, it was a very painful episode to live through, so intense was the deprivation and threat to her identity as a practising Christian. In the sessions, as we focused on this state of affairs, I was filled with a huge anger on her (and probably my own) behalf, which was fuelled by the helplessness that we both experienced through our inability to improve the situation.

This experience helped me to understand that it was also necessary for me to reach a real acceptance of Anne's problems, and my inability to help change the basic problem had to be acknowledged. Up until that point I had thought that this had already been accomplished, but my transference and countertransference experiences revealed otherwise. Anne was also able to express her anger at her lot in life, its unfairness and unremitting daily struggle. It was important to allow her to experience the depths of her despair, and to stay with the helplessness, while not giving up hope of a resolution. The line between acceptance and hope is a fine one, and both aspects need to be held in balance. In the event, a resolution was found when Anne talked to her parish priest who advised her to talk with the bishop. It was then agreed that Anne could be offered, instead of the Host, a drop or two of wine on a teaspoon, which she could, with care, manage to swallow. This was acceptable to all concerned, and Anne felt restored to the life of the church.

The threat of suicide and the sometimes overwhelming need to seek a final resolution to seemingly intractable problems was something I held in mind throughout this period. Anne and I had both taken part in a piece of qualitative research that was undertaken by a colleague, Patti Wallace, in 1989, in which it was found that a high percentage of ill or disabled people had suicidal thoughts but often found it necessary to protect their counsellors from that knowledge. Anne and I had discussed this on occasions and had agreed that it was important to acknowledge that a person can have thoughts about ending her or his life, while at the same time her or his faith or concern for others might prevent her or him acting on their impulses. The understanding that life's experiences can be bad enough at times to make an individual feel like ending it all is in itself therapeutic.

* * *

In the spring of 1995, after some discussion, we agreed to meet fortnightly, as Anne felt she would like to see if she could manage a longer space in between sessions. This was with a view to working towards an ending. It meant we had to move to the main building where we could use my office, which I also used for counselling. Space was tight in the William Kyle Centre at WPF, which was a building that had been adapted for disabled people, and the room we had used there was needed for weekly sessions.

Anne had to negotiate a flight of stairs to my office, not without some difficulty, which made me nervous but amused Anne, who, I think, felt that I was fussing unnecessarily—and she was probably right!

This arrangement worked quite well, but the following year Anne's father was ill, and in November 1996 he was found to have cancer. He died in May 1997 after a comparatively short illness. Anne had got on well with her father, but their relationship had not always been an easy one because she had been unsure as to how he felt about her disability. After his death, we recommenced weekly sessions as we both felt that, with the added dimension of grief, it would benefit Anne to have the space to express her sadness. As with any death, it resonated with past losses, in particular that of Anne's brother Joseph who had been admitted to an institution at age of 14 years following a bout of meningitis that had left him brain-damaged. He remained in hospital for nearly twenty years, although initially he was able to go home for weekends. During that time Anne visited him regularly, even when he failed to recognize her. This contact enabled Anne to act as an intermediary between the hospital and her family. It also gave her some understanding of her parents' feelings towards their two disabled children, and it allowed her own strengths to emerge. Anne mourned the loss of these two important members of her family, and she was able to feel more positively towards her father as a result. Joseph and Anne did not spend a lot of time together as children, but they were taken to Lourdes together when they were quite young, and they went again when Joseph was 11 and Anne was 14. Anne remembered this visit well, as Joseph was taken ill there following an epileptic fit. Later, Joseph became blind and his condition deteriorated. This caused Anne and the family a lot of pain. They paid a final visit to Lourdes in 1981 with an organization that helped disabled people, and Joseph died in 1983. Anne often spoke about Joseph and the special relationship they had; when her father died, she felt reassured that they would be reunited in their faith, as father and son.

After six months we resumed our fortnightly sessions, and we began to think about ending. I was reducing my hours at WPF, and we agreed that Anne would continue to see me in my private practice, on the basis of need. This arrangement worked quite well, and Anne managed the journey out to Wimbledon when an issue arose that she wanted to discuss or work on.

* * *

When I finally left London, Anne was more than able to manage her own life, with its ups and downs. She continued to study with the Open University and planned a visit to Australia, where one of her carers came from. Anne had an abundance of emotional strength, acquired through many years of striving to cope with her numerous physical difficulties, and a generosity of spirit that enabled her to find meaning in some of the most difficult of life's circumstances.

CHAPTER ELEVEN

Who am I, that I might become?
The spiritual dimension in work with people who are seriously physically ill

Judy Parkinson

When someone is diagnosed with a life-threatening ill-ness, one of the questions in his or her mind is likely to be, "why me?". The question might not be voiced to anyone else, or it may be asked directly—of a doctor, a nurse, a friend, a psychotherapist, or God.

In this chapter, I focus on the spiritual dimension in the dia-logue between patient and therapist in the situation of the patient becoming, or having been, seriously physically ill. The "spiritual" embraces questions of meaning, purpose, existence, and mortality, for the patient and also for the psychotherapist. The life-threaten-ing conditions I am thinking about here include those illnesses such as cancer, heart disease, stroke, and AIDS that follow a course through from diagnosis to treatment and may, or may not, be pro-gressive and terminal.

I shall begin by briefly considering what spirituality means in our Western culture. I then discuss how the spiritual enters into and affects both the dialogue and the relationship between patient and therapist. My aim is to think about how we as therapists work with a dimension of human experience that, in face-to-face conversation, is often neglected, ignored, or avoided. The "spiritual" can seem to be embarrassing, frightening, or too personal to be enquired into, and it can also be felt to be important, interesting, or fascinating. Thinking about such a topic inevitably raises questions.

This chapter aims to explore rather than to answer, but it concentrates—hopefully in a helpful way—on some of the issues that can arise in the course of clinical work that seeks to allow for the spirituality of the patient to be expressed.

At the outset I want to acknowledge that the thoughts and views discussed here, whether quoted from other sources or arising from my own clinical experience and practice, may differ from those of the readers of this chapter. Our spiritual life is a personal one, and there will be as many definitions of spirituality and ways of expressing our spiritual selves as there are individuals.

What is spirituality?

In the autumn of 2004 a story in *The Times* newspaper was headlined, "Horoscopes Are New Religion" (18 September). In an edition of the "Body and Soul" section of *The Times* (9 October 2004), the leading article, entitled "A light in the darkness", began: "Are you unhappy, confused, frightened, stuck, mildly dissatisfied—or do you simply fancy the latest inspirational sensation? Consult a guru. It's the modern way." The writer went on to list the various sorts of gurus we consult: "life-style gurus, spiritual gurus, intimacy gurus, business gurus, mind gurus".

At the beginning of the twenty-first century, we are living in a postmodern age. What is real, what is true, what is absolute is no longer assumed or taken for granted. Theories and ideologies are questioned, values are shifting, and old, established ways of thinking are turned over, to be re-worked.

Art, science, philosophy, architecture, fashion, and style are all "postmodern." This "cultural soup" (O'Donnell, 2003) is potentially confusing, but it does allow for variety, creativity, and individual expression. It is a very different form of culture from that of the pre- and post-war years of the twentieth century.

In those times, a serious discussion about spirituality would probably have centred around a religious or faith theme. In our multicultural, multi-faith society, the word "spiritual" relates not only to traditional religious practices, but to New-Age philosophies and to our current emphasis on the development of the individual person, mind, body, and spirit.

Spirituality is a difficult word to define because an attempt to be all-inclusive will lead to vagueness and a definition that is too specific may be limiting. The *Oxford English Dictionary* defines spiritual as "1) of, relating to, or affecting the human spirit as opposed to material or physical things". Spirit is defined as "1) the non-physical part of a person which is the seat of emotions and character". In accordance with this, Samuels, Shorter, and Plaut (1986) refer to Jung as having "applied the word 'spirit' to the non-material aspect of a living person . . ." (p. 140). The living, moving, vital person is made up of mind, body, soul, and spirit. The spirit can be thought of as part of the essence, or the essential being, of each person.

The spirituality of the person can find expression through formal religious or non-religious ceremony, within the context of a group or community, or through solitary prayer, meditation, or reflection.

The subject of contemplation can be the "other", in the transpersonal realm: God, or gods. Or, in the intra- or interpersonal realms, "god" might be perceived as within oneself or within another. The experience of beauty in art, literature, or music can be spiritually uplifting, while the wonder and awesomeness of creation, witnessed in nature, can bring us into a humble relation to things bigger and more powerful than our small selves.

Spirituality can be explored in relation to the political, cultural, and social life of the individual or the collective (Samuels, 2001). It does not confine itself to being relevant to the good or the holy. Rather, "Spirituality is not only a matter of maturity or individuation; it also resides in confusion, suffering and immaturity" (Samuels 2001, p. 128).

Who am I . . . ?

> "The basic anxiety, the anxiety of a finite being about the threat
> of non-being, cannot be eliminated. It belongs to existence
> itself."
>
> Paul Tillich (1952, p. 48)

According to the theologian and philosopher Paul Tillich, ontological anxiety is "the state in which a being is aware of its possible
non-being" (Tillich, 1952, p. 44). What does non-being mean ? For
human beings, the question of who we are and the search for our
own individual identity is fundamental to our existence. At the
most profound and basic level of our being, we cannot survive
unless we know that we exist and that we are meaningful.

We discover who we are only in relation to another being, and
we can know ourselves only because we have been known: "When
I look I am seen, so I exist" (Winnicott, 1971, p. 114).

Many of us can recall times throughout our lives, from childhood on, when we have felt, or been made to feel, that we are "not
there". Experiences of exclusion in the school playground, of not
being chosen to be a member of the team, are painful and may affect us emotionally long after the event. As adults we may feel un-
acknowledged in some way, "unseen", or unrecognized by others.
No matter how generally secure we are in our own identity, there
are times when we know the anxiety of the threat of non-being—a
mental or physical threat to the continuing existence and recognition of the "person I am".

When someone discovers he or she is seriously ill, all that has
been secure and predictable in that person's life becomes subject
to change and to the unknown. The person is thrust into the world
of illness. The routine of daily life is disrupted, and this may have
immediate financial or social consequences. Someone who has,
reasonably and confidently, taken him/herself and his or her roles
in life for granted may now feel fearful and undermined, not secure in knowing who he or she is or what is expected of him or
her. The person who has never contemplated his or her own death
is now faced with the possibility of not recovering from the illness.
Not surprisingly, this situation can amount to an existential crisis,
and, as I have written about elsewhere, the sense of a secure self
can be severely shaken (Parkinson, 2003).

Following the diagnosis and after the initial shock of hearing bad news, there is a period of emotional and psychological adjustment. During this time people will react differently, according to their individual personalities and circumstances. Some will express emotions such as anger or fear; others will withdraw emotionally; others may become more than usually assertive or more than usually vulnerable.

A period of psychological retreat, whatever form this takes, can be a necessary survival strategy and helpful to the vulnerable ego, as mental adjustments are made and ways of coping with the situation found. An ill person will often reflect on his or her life, present and past, and may need the supportive understanding of a therapist to help him or her talk through (and sometimes recall) past events such as periods of time spent in hospital, the death of loved ones, or other traumas that are revived by the present experience and may have a bearing on how the individual copes emotionally.

Victor Frankl (1984) writes that "Man's search for meaning is the primary motivation in his life" (p. 121). As we go through life, we attempt to make sense of ourselves and of the people and the world around us, seeking meaning and, from this, a sense of purpose. This is a lifelong task. Faced with the ultimate—the possibility of death—the present takes on a new and different perspective. Things that once had priority, such as money and material possessions, now take second place to the importance of good and lasting, loving relationships with other people. I have been struck and sometimes humbled by how people, often young, describe the changes in attitude that have taken place in themselves following diagnosis and the start of a period of illness and treatment.

Priorities change, very quickly for some, and there is often a kind of wisdom that comes from seeing life in a new light.

. . . that I might become?

> "What is REAL ?" asked the rabbit one day, when they were lying side by side near the nursery fender, . . . "It doesn't happen all at once," said the Skin Horse. "You become. It takes a long time."

> Margery Williams, *The Velveteen Rabbit* (2004)

In conversation with the counsellor or psychotherapist, the subject of the patient's spirituality may arise spontaneously and naturally, or it may be touched upon cautiously by the patient and left to see how the therapist responds. I can think of examples of patients, talking about their spirituality, who have spoken generally, "I see myself as being a spiritual kind of a person", and quite specifically: "I think that God must be punishing me." Several patients have said something along the lines of: "I am not a religious person, but I do pray." These statements are often spoken in the context of the person trying to come to his or her own understanding of what is happening and can be revealing of a process of change, as the individual finds him/herself reflecting on the "before" and "after" of the period of illness.

Changes in the person's attitudes towards his or her life and other people around him or her may be discerned in a different or new perspective on his or her own spirituality. Patients may talk about searching for a faith or belief that can sustain them in the present and give them comfort when thinking about their own death. Some may rediscover a faith left behind in the form of child-hood memories of being taken to church or singing religious songs. Some have lapsed, and they begin to feel they want to re-establish old religious practices or rituals.

Some question their existing faith, and others may lose their faith or go through a "wilderness experience", what St John of The Cross called the "dark night of the soul". There is a search for hope—"Something that will keep me going"—and there may be fear—"I do not know where I am going."

These questions, put to the therapist, might, in a different situation or at a different time, have been talked over with a priest, a spiritual director, or a religious leader in the individual's particular faith community. The therapist may temporarily take the place of or represent the priest for the patient, who will hope that the therapist will be able to be sensitive to and try to understand something of the struggle that the patient is engaged in.

* * *

I shall now describe, in a condensed form and without comment at this point, something of the work that took place over a period of two years with a young man who had AIDS. I hope to illustrate how the mental, emotional, and spiritual life of a person who suddenly finds himself facing his own deterioration and, in this case death, can change and develop.

Mark, as I will call him, was 32 years old when, in the space of one week, he was diagnosed as being HIV-positive and as having AIDS-related pneumonia. Doctors told him that he could expect to live for between fifteen to twenty-four months.

When I met him, a few weeks after he had been given this news, he was shocked, frightened, and angry. He had been a successful businessman, and he said that the diagnosis of AIDS had completely changed his life.

He had always been optimistic and looked to the future. He set himself goals and worked up to fifteen hours a day in order to achieve those goals. Now, he said, he had no future but death. Death was his goal.

Mark's father had been a professional sportsman. Mark had the same talent, but an accident early on in his training had forced him to give up any hope of making a career out of his abilities. He bitterly regretted losing the opportunity to use his gifts and to become a star like his father, with whom he had an intensely competitive relationship. Instead, he put all his available energies into an alternative occupation and, at the point of diagnosis, was travelling around the world making business contacts as well as leading a full social life, much of this in the gay scene.

As his initial shock wore off and he was less acutely frightened, he became depressed. Because he was unwell and could not travel, he lost his job and, with it, his self-esteem. He became preoccupied with death. During the day he watched anything on television that was remotely connected to the subject of death, and at night he had horrible dreams in which he would see what he called "images of death": skeletons, corpses, ghosts. He was frightened, most of all, by what he imagined as the process of dying—becoming socially isolated, a burden to others, shunned by those who would not want to be near him if he developed a skin condition associated with AIDS.

Mark was brought up as a Roman Catholic, but he stopped attending Mass as soon as he was able to make up his own mind about whether he wanted to go to church. He had no interest in religion as such, but he told me that he believed in "a God of some sort".

One day he came through the grounds of the convent in which the Westminster Pastoral Foundation buildings are situated, passing a nun as he walked. He associated me with this religious place, and he thought I might be a Catholic. In the session, he said that he was thinking I must do my job for my own self-satisfaction, as it would help me to feel good about myself. Something like, he continued, doing my work as a penance. I did not need to do more than think about whether he may be attributing bad feelings about himself to me, as he then talked about regretting his promiscuous lifestyle and the consequences of this for both himself and his family.

He became concerned to make his peace with God. He did not want to go to church, because he felt he might be judged for being gay or made to feel that AIDS was a punishment from God. He wanted to talk to God, but he did not know how to go about this and thought it would have to be through going to see his local priest, a man whom he did not know. He felt that the only way that anyone could communicate with God was through a human being who had the authority to address God directly.

We had talked a lot about Mark's frustration with his father's apparent lack of interest in his son's welfare and Mark's hurt that his father did not seem to want to (or to be able to) talk with him about his illness, despite the extreme seriousness of his condition. I questioned his idea that he could not talk directly with God.

I said that he had been feeling he could not talk directly to his earthly father and he had needed the help of another human being, me, to think about how he could communicate to his father in any way at all. Did he feel that God and his father must be similar?

He thought about this, and he went to see his local priest. He established some contact on an ad-hoc basis, forming a good rapport with a man he could talk to and who came to stand for a less persecuting version of the church and its "fathers". A few months before he died, Mark told me about what he called "pre-dreams" that he had while lying in bed at night. He imagined meeting St Peter at the gates of Paradise and being "ushered into the gay quarter", in which there would be lush green tennis courts and sparkling blue swimming pools. He enjoyed these fantasies because he thought that if he could not be a star on earth, he had a chance of being one in heaven.

Sadly, Mark and his father never found a way to communicate with each other. Neither did Mark feel able to talk to his mother, who had suffered several mental breakdowns and he felt she needed to be protected from knowing about the seriousness of his condition. He did, however, form a relationship with his grandfather, who was also dying. They talked to each other by telephone, and Mark felt that they had a good understanding of each other, which he found reassuring, and this helped him to cope with his fears of dying. He told me that dying felt like "a kid going into a sweet shop and seeing all the sweets there but only having five minutes to choose them—so he takes all he can".

In the last few months of his life, Mark wanted to help other people as much as he could. He volunteered to be a driver for patients with AIDS who needed to be taken to and from their hospital appointments, knowing that soon he would be as ill as they were and appreciating the chance to be useful while he was still able. This gave him a sense of purpose.

I had learnt a great deal from Mark in the time we had met, and, although I could not predict then the context or the time, I felt that I was very likely to want to write about him. After discussing this with my colleagues, I asked Mark, in a session, if he would give me his permission to write about some of what we had talked about together. I told him how much I had appreciated and valued his openness and honesty in talking with me and that he had given me much precious insight into how a person who is dying feels and thinks. Mark was delighted. He imagined people reading about him, and then he said he wanted to help other people to understand what it was like to die at a young age, maybe to help take the fear away.

Not long after this, I sat with Mark and I looked at his expression. There was a change. His bright blue eyes had become dull, and there was a faraway expression in them that I had never seen before. He knew he was dying, and he knew that I had sensed that he would not be coming to see me for much longer. I saw a light go out in his eyes that day. He died a few days later.

Spirituality and the psychotherapist

> "Those who do not run away from our pains but touch them
> with compassion bring healing and new strength."
>
> Nouwen (1990, p. 38)

It is not only our general culture that has moved into a postmodern age in the last fifty years.

The discipline of psychotherapy has developed in parallel, allowing new ideas and approaches to be thought about and practised. The spiritual and religious side of the mental life of the person has begun to be taken more into consideration, encouraging debate and writings on the subject by psychotherapists of all traditions. To some extent, depth psychology has left behind the suspicion of religion characteristic of the Freudian era. Contemporary Freudians, along with contemporary Jungians, as well as others in the psychoanalytic tradition, are involved in the debate, indicating a willingness to incorporate this subject into the theoretical and clinical arena (e.g., see Black, 2000; Clark, 1998; Field, 2005).

In the same way that some psychotherapists have developed an interest in the spiritual life of the person and have trained as spiritual directors, so some priests have trained in counselling or psychotherapy. In Britain, groups such as the Association for Pastoral and Spiritual Care and Counselling (a division of the British Association for Counselling and Psychotherapy) have an important part to play in offering a forum for discussion.

There is potential for both a crossover and conflict of roles between psychotherapist and priest, and the differences between the professions need to be both understood and respected in order to maintain their individual identities.

In the conversations I had with Mark, the concerns raised were of a profoundly spiritual and theological nature. We discussed questions of hope, eternity, forgiveness, and the existence and personality of God. Had I been a priest, the direction of the conversations would probably have been weighted differently from the beginning, more towards an exploration of Mark's spiritual life and being. As it was, the question I had to consider was how to respect and acknowledge the existence of both his spiritual and psychological concerns without either reducing his spiritual searching to something that could be explained away in psychological terms or, on the other hand, not giving enough attention to the emotional content of his spiritual worries.

How the therapist chooses to respond to the patient's wish or need to explore his or her spirituality will depend upon such factors as the therapist's theoretical orientation or bias, preferred way of working, personality, and personal background. Consultation with a supervisor or colleagues can be a vital means of support. In some settings in which I have both trained and worked, it has been possible to talk, over a long period of time, with groups of trusted colleagues who have had similar therapeutic interests and goals and who have wished to acknowledge the importance of the spiritual side of our psychic life, allowing for diversity and difference as a potent means of learning.

There is then the question of how to think about what the patient is saying. How do we respond, for instance, to the patient who says, "I think God is punishing me"? There is no right or wrong answer, but there are questions to consider. Do we think in terms of the state of the person's internal-object relations? How are these changed or modified or worsened by his or her current situation? An already persecutory inner world might become temporarily even more threatening during a period of illness. The illness itself can become a persecutory object, or the experience of pain or some treatments can become persecutory in quality. Is the patient depressed? It can be important that the therapist is alert to this very understandable possibility and recognizes that the statement might be a reflection of a depressive state of mind that needs to be recognized and taken seriously, particularly if there is a risk of suicide. The statement might be seen as a way in to allowing the patient to talk about the meaning he or she is attributing to becoming ill. Two examples come to mind.

> One woman, in her early fifties, who had breast cancer, told me she believed that God was punishing her for past "sins". Talking with her in detail about what she meant revealed that she was preoccupied with what she felt were wrongdoings she had committed, or been tempted to commit, in the course of her life. She had a strong faith in God, and she was burdened by feelings of regret and a desire to put things right with God before she died. Although I offered her the opportunity to talk about what was bothering her so much, she declined, feeling

that she needed to talk to a priest and confess what she saw as her wrongdoings. I referred her to the hospital chaplain, and she developed a close and supportive relationship with him; this helped her, eventually, to die feeling much more at peace with herself and her God.

Recently I talked with another woman, of the same age and also with breast cancer. In the first session she suddenly said, "I must have done something bad in my past lives to have got this disease". I asked her what she meant, adding a question as to whether she believed in other lifetimes. She said: "Oh no, I don't mean reincarnation or anything like that—I just mean that so many bad things have happened to me in my life, one thing after another, that I think, why another bad thing? It all seems to have happened to me." This patient felt that her whole life had been blighted, as though she had done something wrong. She did not have a religious belief, nor did she feel she had done something actually wrong. She did feel, however, out of control of events occurring in her life, and in her despair she felt that things would never go right for her in her lifetime.

Finally, I shall return to Mark and the intervention I made in the form of the question I decided to put to him. The question was: did he feel he could talk to God directly?

Over the two years we met, I became very fond of Mark, who I found charming, lively, funny, brash, and arrogant. I was conscious, all along, of my concern for him and of the possibility that my feelings of anxiety, distress, and anger on his behalf could interfere with my objectivity. The support of a group of colleagues in a close-knit supervision group was invaluable in helping me to cope with these feelings. Talking about them enabled me to recognize when my emotional reactions were stemming from my own anxieties concerning illness and death, in partial identification with Mark, and when they were responsive to feelings that he was communicating, both consciously and unconsciously.

His wish to talk to God, ignored since his childhood recognition of Him and then turning away, was heartfelt. Whatever my own beliefs might have been, I wanted to help him to find a relationship with the God he envisaged, which I recognized might be able to be different from his relationship with his earthly father. I had to ask myself whether it was right to convey an understanding of the transferential anxieties involved in his fears about approaching the authoritarian figure of God-in-his-mind and leave this as an "interpretation" in the classical psychoanalytic sense. Alternatively, I could ask a question that might indicate my own beliefs or that would address his thoughts that I was a Catholic, possibly a nun, and so representative of religious figures in his past. In the end, by in effect suggesting that he might be able to talk to God directly, I think I did all of these. My immediate aim, however, was to try to help him to find what, at that point in his life he needed to find—his own, individual relationship with someone, a being, that he came to call God.

Counselling someone who is ill and who may die as a result of the illness can be mentally and emotionally demanding of the therapist in ways that are particular to this kind of work. The therapist may identify with the patient on the grounds of age or background. There may be personal and painful reminders of experiences of illness or of the death of people close to the therapist. Working with such raw anxieties as the fear of death and the loss of the person, "me", can arouse strong feelings that may threaten to overwhelm the therapist. He or she may want to idealize the patient, to "run away" by distancing or withdrawing, or to compensate for feelings of helplessness by becoming "chronically nice" in reaction to the "disturbingly not-nice" feelings aroused by a patient's deterioration or impending death (Speck, 1944, p. 97).

Good supervision and, ideally, access to a group of supportive and experienced colleagues can go a long way towards helping the therapist to work effectively by using his or her feelings and thoughts as tools for helping the patient. The ordinary human reactions stirred in us by our patient's situations will underline our capacity to empathize and to feel compassion. Unless we allow ourselves to be affected by our patients, we cannot enter into an experience that, I believe, can be as much a part of the process of our own "becoming" as we are privileged to witness taking place in our patients.

We can only work as best as we can—with the skills that we have, without intrusion, and with humanity—to help our patients to find their own ways to their own becoming. In this, we, too, can grow and learn, and change.

CHAPTER TWELVE

Inner worlds—outer realities. The dying person in counselling and psychotherapy

Ruth Archer

Death is still a relatively taboo subject at the beginning of the twenty-first century, although this is gradually changing. However, for many people it is still a difficult subject to talk about, both before and after the event. The emphasis in the media of defying age and attempting to look younger than we are contributes to the illusion that we can defeat the one certainty in life that we are born with: that one day we will die.

In the nineteenth century, most people died at home surrounded by their family, including the children, from whom they parted in a meaningful way. The funeral was an occasion for neighbours to show their respects by closing their curtains. As the funeral cortege moved through the streets, people stood silently and men removed their hats. Funeral wakes were commonplace, and even the poorest families were anxious to give their relatives "a good send off".

During the twentieth century, these customs were gradually eroded. More and more people died not at home but in hospitals, where they were cared for by nursing staff. The advent of the hospice movement after the Second World War began to replace home or hospital care for some people. They continue to provide a quiet, comfortable environment in which a person can spend his or her last days and take his or her leave of life.

However, death has largely been taken out of the hands of the family and been put into the hands of professionals. The result of these social changes means that some adults in their middle years or older have had little experience of death in their midst, apart from what they have seen on TV or read in the newspapers. They may never have seen the body of a dead person, or been with a relative or friend in their dying moments. Death is an unknown experience for many, and therapists are no exception, which means that they may be ill prepared for working with a person who is facing death.

It is unusual, although not impossible, for patients to present themselves for therapy for the first time, when they have an illness from which they do not expect to recover. Most therapists who encounter terminal illness in a client do so when they have already worked with that person for some time, and the therapeutic alliance will be well established.

The therapist and patient may have already been through the other stages of the illness—the diagnosis, treatment, and emotional impact of this change in life's circumstances—all of which may or may not have prepared the two people for the final stage.

Role of the therapist

The role of the therapist whose patient is terminally ill is in some ways unchanged and in other ways quite different. The pattern of therapy when the patient is physically well is to work towards an ending at the appropriate time and then to say goodbye. The hope is that the person will go on to live his or her life in a more fulfilling manner, but we may not ever know the final outcome of that therapeutic encounter. Therapy with a dying person has a definite outcome, although the timing of the ending may not be predictable—in fact, it is often very uncertain. It is therefore quite important for the therapist and her or his patient to have some idea as to how this final stage is to be managed. This requires some thought at an earlier stage of the person's illness, which is not always easy, particularly if the patient is not ready to discuss this. It will be even more difficult if the therapist is unable to face up to the seriousness of the patient's condition, as this will deprive her or his patient of an opportunity to be part of the decision making. For the therapist, the big question is: "How long should I go on seeing this person." The answer to this is best found in discussion with the individual concerned, as it may mean home or hospital visits. However, some therapists and patients may prefer to end before this stage is reached, while the patient can still come to the consulting-room, before he or she is hospitalized or too ill to travel. It may be possible in these circumstances for the therapist to arrange with the patient that she or he be informed when the patient dies, by a friend or relative. This is a delicate piece of negotiation, but one that may be more satisfactory to both parties than leaving the ending unmarked. However, whether this happens may depend on the quality of the therapeutic relationship, the resolution of the transference, and the stage at which the terminal illness is reached. Sometimes death steals a march on us, leaving us no time to prepare or make plans for a "good-enough" ending.

During a long-term therapeutic relationship, when trust has been established, the news of a patient's serious illness will come as a shock to both people concerned and will alter the course of the therapy. At first, a defence of denial may become a refuge for the therapist as well as the patient until he or she has had time to accommodate this unwelcome piece of news. It is not unknown for the therapist to feel inadequate for the task at this point, and she or he may think about ending before the patient reaches the terminal stage, especially if the prognosis is poor or the disease is progressing rapidly. The age of both parties is another factor, particularly if the patient is young, or around the same age as the therapist or one of her or his children.

The impending death of another is a sure reminder of our own mortality. It confronts us with the possibility that if it can happen to one of our patients, it can happen to us. If the therapist is unacquainted with death, the anxiety surrounding it is often increased, as it constellates the fear of the unknown. The concern of the therapist about being psychically available for the client is also present in these circumstances, and the importance of supervision cannot be overemphasized.

The physical care of the patient is, of course, in the hands of others. Relatives, friends, and professional carers all have a relationship with the ill person that makes them central to the client's well-being. Physical illness needs emotional tending, and this is the domain of the therapist, although everyone concerned with the patient will be emotionally involved, particularly close relatives and friends who are facing the loss of their loved one.

If the patient and therapist decide to continue to work together throughout the course of the client's illness, the therapist will need to be sensitive to the appropriate time to gradually withdraw from transferential work, or at least reduce the number of transference interpretations, depending on the client's ability to still make use of them. It is usually necessary for the therapist to let go of some of the aspirations they previously held for the client, either conscious or unconscious, in order to allow the focus of the work to change, should it become necessary. As the illness progresses, the client will have less energy to invest in the therapy than previously. His or her energy needs to be directed and saved for the task he or she is now faced with, which is facing his or her own death, with its essential loss, together with the need to deal with any pressing unfinished business, although this is not always possible to achieve. The two processes are not necessarily in opposition, but the therapist's awareness of the client's changing needs is paramount.

Both client and therapist will, at this stage, need to engage with both her or his inner and the client's outer reality in a new way. Hospital investigations or difficult treatments may interrupt the pattern of the sessions, and the patient's absence should not automatically be seen as a sign of resistance, even though it may be present to some degree, and may need to be explored.

In his paper "The Ailment" (1957), Tom Main comments that "the sufferer who frustrates a keen therapist by failing to improve is always in danger of meeting primitive human behaviour disguised as treatment". Although Main is referring to a group of people working in a psychiatric hospital setting, we would do well to note these cautionary words, by carefully monitoring our responses to our very ill patients. The therapist's reparative needs may be frustrated by the patient's failure to get physically well, as will his omnipotent phantasies of somehow being able

to cure the patient by psychological means. Feelings of helplessness and the anger that may accompany them may be difficult
to acknowledge because of their unacceptable nature, which is
contrary to the self-image we have of ourselves as therapists. The
therapist's felt need to "abandon ship" may be fuelled by our own
survival needs as well as the patient's projected need to remove
him/herself from the position he or she finds him/herself in. The
emotional responses of the therapist will be influenced by her or
his past experiences of death and bereavement and by what she
or he believes about life, both before and after death. The grieving
process for what has been lost from the therapy, linked as it is with
the actual loss of the person of the client, probably begins when
the therapist is able to accept the irrevocable nature of the person's
condition. At the same time, there may be unexpected opportunities brought into focus by the patient's physical condition which
allow exploration of areas of the person's life that have previously
been inaccessible.

Home or hospital visits

If the therapist and patient decide to go on working together,
it is important to think about how to proceed when the patient
becomes too ill to travel to the therapist's consulting-room. If
the patient agrees to home visits, the boundary issues need to be
thought through before a visit is made. It is almost inevitable that
the therapist will meet other family members or friends, if only
when they open the door. Because the therapist is entering into
the client's social space, a boundary has already been expanded.
In this situation, often either the patient or a relative, bound by the
unspoken rules of hospitality, will offer a cup of tea or coffee when
the therapist arrives as a visitor. If the therapist would prefer not
to enter into this social situation, this can be clarified beforehand.
It has been my experience that most people understand that the
patient and therapist need to have privacy and be free from inter-
ruptions during the therapeutic hour. However, should the district
nurse or other persons involved in the patient's care arrive, they
would normally expect to have access to the patient, and the ses-

sion would be interrupted. If nursing visits are regular, it should be possible to negotiate a different time. Some people have pets, and these can be a distraction—particularly if the dog or cat objects to the therapist sitting in its favourite chair!

Hospital visits are less easy to manage because, unless they are told otherwise, ward staff generally suppose that all visitors are friends or relatives. Unless the patient has a single room, or another room is available and the patient is mobile enough to get there, other people and their relatives will be in close proximity, and it is not usually possible to have a session as such in those circumstances. Sometimes appropriate arrangements can be negotiated beforehand, but on the whole it is probably best to keep the visit as brief as the occasion warrants, if this can be agreed with the patient. Each individual situation is different and there are few guidelines, but generally speaking the purpose of the visit is to maintain contact with the client during what might be a long and difficult period of treatment. It must, however, be for the client's benefit rather than the therapist's, who must guard against being intrusive. If she or he does visit the hospital or hospice, the therapist will need to think about how to maintain her or his professional status rather than slipping into the role of friend, bearing in mind that meeting the client outside the consulting-room will feel strange to the client also, and the reason for doing so should be clear and agreed by both parties. Visiting the client at home or in hospital raises issues of time and money, which also have to be agreed. Because it is the therapist who is travelling, an additional cost is involved and needs to be taken into account before embarking on this course of action.

> I visited a patient at home for nearly six months, during the terminal stage of an AIDS-related illness. The patient was estranged from his family and relied on a number of carers to look after him. After a period of trial and error, we arranged that I would visit at a time when he was usually alone, although one of his friends usually waited to let me in. I was able to fit this visit in on my way to work at the WPF, thus avoiding too much extra travel. As the client was on benefits, the fee remained the same. We were able to maintain the newly

established boundaries, and I tried always to arrive and leave on time. We were rarely interrupted, apart from the occasional chance caller, and I declined any refreshment, which was, I felt, one way of maintaining my role. The client had been very keen to continue his therapy, and, looking back, it was a rather profound time for both of us. I saw him on the day before he died, and on that occasion I held his hand, saying little, until it was time to take my leave. We had agreed that I would attend his funeral, which he had arranged, and it seemed important for that continuity to be established. He was not a follower of any particular faith, but he took some comfort from nature's cycle of death and renewal that he observed from his window, through the autumn and winter of one year's end into the spring of another. The work we did over the last few months was limited by his physical weakness, and my role changed to that of a witness, which seemed to be important, particularly in the absence of family members. It was as if the witnessing of his last days of life by another person somehow validated their meaning.

In the service our general policy was to go on seeing the person until the end of his or her life, if that is what the patient wanted, thus avoiding abandoning him or her at a very vulnerable time. This was often costly for the therapist and required a realistic appraisal of both the patient's outer reality and the therapist's own inner resources as well as an understanding of the patient's inner world.

For these reasons, we rarely saw people for the first time when they were terminally ill, as there was little time to establish a therapeutic alliance. Also, it would often have necessitated a home or hospital visit. Occasionally, we were able to comply with a request to visit a very ill person at home, and I can recall one counsellor who visited an elderly Asian lady, for about five sessions, before she died from a heart condition. Mrs K, who was a widow, was extremely distressed by the thought of dying so far from her home. Her daughter had also been present for some of the time, after newly arriving in this country, and it seemed as if the counsellor's intervention was felt to be of some benefit to them both, in such difficult circumstances.

I also saw one of two elderly sisters for about eight weeks before she died, when she was in her mid-eighties. The work was centred on her need to "clear out the cupboard" that she perceived her life to be, which I took to be a metaphor for "putting her house in order", although at the time neither she nor I were consciously aware that she was terminally ill. She died quite suddenly, when she was, I think, ready and, I hope, at peace. Her sister came to tell me of this a few weeks later, after I had written to enquire after her whereabouts. I then had five sessions with her sister, who was the only surviving member of the family and needed a little help to face that fact and adjust to living alone for the first time in her life, in her eighty-second year.

The patient's view

It may take some time for people to accept the fact that they have a condition from which they are unlikely to recover. Some people may never consciously reach that stage, even though they are very unwell and all the signs indicate that they are not getting better. It is as if the mind needs to protect itself from the knowledge of impending death, until the person is ready to cope with it.

> I knew a long-distance lorry driver who talked every day about his next trip abroad, even when he was too weak to get out of bed, right up until the day before he died, when he lapsed into a coma. His family colluded with this, as it seemed to be what he wanted, after his son had suggested that it might be a while before he could take to the road and was indignantly rebuffed.

> A colleague who was an experienced nurse was terminally ill from secondary lung cancer, but she did not recognize this until about ten days before she died, as she was convinced she was suffering from a bad bout of bronchitis. She had had surgery for the primary cancer, a few years earlier, and had faced that with courage and made a good recovery. When she became ill again, it took much longer for her to realize the implications of her illness; although her family were aware, they felt unable to talk about it until she was ready to hear it.

The reverse can also happen. Sometimes it is the relatives who are unable to accept the diagnosis, and want to protect themselves and their loved one from the truth.

> I worked for about three months with a terminally ill woman in her late fifties. She and her husband were devoted to each other, but they had a stiff-upper-lip attitude to life and found it difficult to talk about their feelings. The husband took great care of his wife, driving her to and from the sessions, and was busy making plans for a holiday abroad, even though it was quite clear that she would be too unwell to travel. She told me about this, adding that she thought it "was pointless"; when I explored this further, she tentatively said that she thought she was dying. I said I felt she was right, and after weeping for a while, she said she felt great relief that the truth of her situation had been acknowledged. "I felt I was going mad," she said. I did not see her again, but I learnt later that she and her husband had gone to see her consultant the next day, who had confirmed that what she suspected was true, enabling the couple to face the situation together.

Terminal illness, when recognized by the patient, brings with it a new set of experiences, both physical and emotional, that have to be accommodated. The difficulties that surround this time may be exacerbated by physical pain or discomfort and the fear of the unknown. Because as a society we are largely unacquainted with the naturalness of death, we struggle to understand what is happening to us, or what we might expect to happen when we die. The "how" of this event often feels more important than the "when", and our personal belief system—whatever it may be—becomes more central to our thinking.

Inevitably, a sense of helplessness, of being caught up in events beyond our control, which we have failed to prevent, brings with it feelings of guilt, shame, and perhaps envy of those not in the same predicament, including the therapist. There is a sense of loss of the ideal self, which may be projected onto the therapist, or mourned, as we come to realize that it cannot be reclaimed. Concern for the people that one will leave behind, particularly if there are dependent children, takes up a great deal of time and energy in the early stages of a terminal illness. Depending on the time span between the onset of the disease and the quality of life before the final stage, it may or may not be possible to accomplish everything that one would like to.

Sometimes people make great efforts to deal with unfinished business, particularly in relationships, when the need for reparation and reconciliation is pressing. This may also apply to friends and relatives, who may want to get something "off their chest" before it is too late. It is often helpful for the patient to talk about his or her life, what he or she has accomplished, and what he or she will have to leave unfinished. The therapist is there to receive these reflections from the patient and to help the patient understand that he or she is valued and respected as a person, particularly if he or she is burdened by guilt, and fearful of retribution, for past actions. To forgive one's self may be difficult but is important in achieving peace of mind before letting go of life.

If the illness has been protracted and painful, death may be welcomed with a sense of relief from suffering, not only for the patient but also his or her relatives.

Taking matters into one's own hands and ending it all, before it becomes too much to bear, is a course considered by many people, even if it is not acted upon. This course of action is against the law, and this may prohibit people from taking their own life, as may concern for close family members or religious belief. The patient may not want to disclose these thoughts to his or her therapist, for many reasons, including the fear of censure; the therapist therefore needs to take particular note of "throw-away lines" that may indicate a need for these fears to be heard.

The majority of people, when faced with the knowledge of their own death, begin to think long thoughts about the meaning of their life, what they might or might not have achieved, and what might lie beyond. Half-forgotten religious beliefs from childhood may be re-examined, or questioned, and these may be tentatively discussed in the therapy. It is not unknown for the patient to ask the therapist what her or his beliefs about life and death are, in an attempt to include the therapist in the experience, not only as a transference figure but as a real person who will at some time be facing a similar fate. This discussion, if allowed to take place, seems to reduce the patient's isolation, as it acknowledges the universality of our human experience. It is important, therefore, for the therapist to have considered this aspect of the patient's journey, if the therapist wishes to stay alongside him or her.

Letting go

The dying process is one of letting go. In a sense, it is the reverse of what happens during the developmental processes of early childhood, which begin with a two-person relationship and gradually widen out to include other family members, then the wider world of school, and so on. At the other end of life, the circle gradually decreases. Terminal illness means giving up work, then other activities, and then social contacts. The number of people in touch with the client is smaller once he or she is confined to his or her home and later, perhaps, bed. These are the external realities that accompany the inner experience of gradually relinquishing even the most ordinary of everyday things—shopping, going to the library, visiting friends, going to the theatre. These activities become memories, as the centre of activity narrows into the daily routine of bodily care.

For some this is an extended process, particularly in chronic illness, but for others it might be comparatively short. In sudden death, there is no time for this gradual process to take place, and the shock and impact of the event leaves no time for anyone to prepare themselves, especially close relatives.

For the therapist, there is also a letting go—initially of the hope of the patient's recovery and resumption of normal life, then of the therapy running an uninterrupted course to its anticipated outcome and ending at a future date, within the established guidelines. Instead, there is another dimension present, with a different ending, over which we will have little control, and which cannot easily be foreseen. This is largely uncharted territory, where we must navigate by the stars and such internal wisdom as we may possess. It is a privilege—uncomfortable, at times daunting, but always awesome—to be present at such a time in another person's life.

Practical matters

During the final period of a person's life, his or her thoughts may turn to the funeral. Some people plan their own funeral in advance, others do not give it much thought. It is helpful if the therapist has some understanding of the patient's wishes as regards her or his attendance at the funeral. The family may also have a view; in my experience, this has always been that it is fitting for the therapist to attend, in recognition of how significant her or his role had been in the patient's life.

If it is possible to discuss this with the client, arrangements can be made as to who will give the therapist the necessary funeral details. It is also an opportunity to discover what the patient feels about the inevitable meeting between the therapist and the patient's friends and family (assuming they have not met previously). The therapist can also reassure the patient that confidentiality continues after death, lest he or she harbours an unspoken concern that the therapist might disclose details of their work together.

Discussion of these matters enables the client to understand that he will be mourned by the therapist, but also reassures that the boundaries will still be maintained. Normally the therapist leaves after the funeral service and would not go on to attend the gathering of family and friends, although she or her may be invited to do so.

Afterwards

The death of a client, even if expected, is a painful event for therapists, who may feel themselves to be more affected than they had imagined they would be. The therapists need to acknowledge their bereavement and allow themselves to grieve. Attending the funeral, if this is possible, is part of this experience, as is taking the opportunity to talk through the experience with colleagues in supervision, where the grieving process can be facilitated. Writing up the notes and closing the file all help to establish the reality of the loss of the therapeutic relationship and the individual person. There may be an issue of an unpaid fee to think about and resolve in a way that feels appropriate to the work and the ending, however that was accomplished.

It is likely however that the experience of being alongside another person prior to his or her death will affect us deeply and enlarge our understanding of this most common but least known-about aspect of human experience.

CHAPTER THIRTEEN

Supervision of counsellors working with seriously physically ill patients

Gertrud Mander

Psychotherapy supervision is practised over a wide field of clinical work dealing with emotional and psychosomatic problems and always needs to be adaptive to specific needs, while focusing on its main task of containing and facilitating the therapeutic couple in their joint work.

Supervising a group of counsellors working with clients suffering from serious physical illness was a challenge that stretched me in many ways and felt daunting as the work was located on the interface of body and psyche, in a dimension where issues of mortality and death were always present, while everyday life and how to manage financially could be difficult for the clients. The counsellors came from various backgrounds. Some had been nurses before they undertook a counsellor training and had the medical knowledge that was useful when dealing with often life-threatening illnesses and with patients on medication for these. Others were experienced psychoanalytic psychotherapists who had chosen the work for its specific interest, for the chance to learn something new and to do something particularly meaningful and reparative, without expecting big rewards, success, or quick striking changes in their clients.

Specifics of the work

All the counsellors found that working with psychic experiences arising from uncontrollable bodily processes was taxing their empathetic responses to the utmost, and they needed the group and the supervision as a secure structure to make them feel strong and safe enough to carry and process powerful emotions and projections encountered in the clinical work. The clients' anxieties and the defences against these were often unconsciously transmitted to the group and sometimes threatened to overwhelm the thinking processes necessary to understand the clients' distress, to remain helpful, and to be compassionate without giving in to hopelessness or depression. There was also a pervasive and powerful dynamic tension between the "healthy" counsellor and the "ill" client which had to be addressed as with any difference, and unconscious fears about the counsellor's own health were liable to interfere with being fully attentive to the clients' illness.

Constructing narratives and life stories

Much of the work was about helping clients tell and understand their life stories, about addressing their difficulties relating to others and the stresses of managing the practical tasks of keeping alive. The counsellors had to curb their spontaneous impulses to reassure and advise, to rein in their strong desires to avoid the clients' angry, aggressive, and difficult emotions, and to understand the complex countertransference reactions that the clients' clinical material produced in them. They had to learn how to stay with what the clients brought, instead of casting about for instant solutions, and in supervision they were encouraged to develop the patience of listening carefully in order to help the clients help themselves, whether in dealing with their mortal fears, with the emotions caused by their practical problems or with underlying issues relating to their relationships and life histories in general.

Clinical situations

There were clients suffering from HIV whose future was uncertain and was overshadowed by the knowledge that their condition was incurable and life would never be normal again. One of them continued to be sexually promiscuous without considering that he might be spreading the virus, in denial of the seriousness of his condition. This created an ethical dilemma for the counsellor, who tried to work with the client's denial psychodynamically. Others could be helped to develop their creative potential by attending art classes and learning to paint and teach, which made them feel alive and able to express themselves. There were multiple sclerosis patients in the early stages of their illness who used the therapeutic alliance to look at the implications of their diagnoses and to prepare, with the support of their counsellors, for the more disabling processes of their developing illness.

Quite a few were crippled by persistent and severe ME, which could not be shifted as the underlying psychic causes remained inaccessible. A few of them learnt to come to terms with their reduced state, whereas others tried to find some meaningful activity with which to break the tedium of their days while they waited for a change in their baffling condition. One of these clients was particularly imaginative, thinking up ingenious projects for recycling objects or staging events for other patients, and she finally came up with the idea of introducing annual opening days for private London squares, which proved successful; however, it was too stressful for her to develop it further herself, whereupon she handed it on to a local charity.

Many clients, who were what the medical profession calls "somatizers", had developed chronic physical conditions like IBS, constipation, or ulcers, which required that they faced unconscious anxieties and conflicts rather than splitting them off and defending against them. Other people were awaiting transplants, major operations, or treatments for cancer and had asked to be helped and held through these traumatic medical interventions. Encouraging them to talk about their fears and being listened to and contained while the crisis lasted was essential, as the clients' serious conditions and symptoms were proof that there was a defensive regression to a primitive state of denial. The counsellors' task was to function as auxiliary egos pre- and post-operatively, and thus they had an important parental role until the clients were able to face their anxieties and to manage by themselves again.

I realized as a supervisor that most of the clients who were seen in the service profited from the counselling in more than one way. By being given weekly support, they experienced that somebody cared sufficiently for them to hold them in mind. This gradually enabled them to feel valued and to make meaningful changes in their ability to relate, in their depressed self-conception, and in their attitude to the conflicted past, the troubled present, and the dark uncertain future. The unusually taxing supervisory work confirmed for me the overall importance of the therapeutic relationship—the supervisor's and the supervisee's—to contain and model emotions too strong to be born alone and to operate dynamically on many levels: the parental, the infantile, the transferential, and the real. In the supervision group, the absent client was the focus of attention, and the reason for being together was to think about and explore his or her physical conditions and emotional problems, while the present counsellor's countertransference, fears, and blind spots provided the material for additional supervisory intervention, support, and challenge.

Looking at defences and parallel processes

The clients' stories and needs were aired and shared in the group, and much work was done by looking at the clients' as well as at the supervisees' defences, which are essential but also blocking and thus require careful scrutiny and monitoring. The group became a container for unusually complex parallel processes operating between the clinical material discussed and the shifting dynamic group processes connecting, splitting, or fusing the members of the group which needed to be creatively interpreted and understood in order for the client work to proceed fruitfully.

It is by now a commonplace that much nursing training in the past was based on building up strong disciplinary defences against primitive anxieties arising in the presence of illness. In a study by Isabel Menzies-Lyth (1988), these procedures were analysed in a hospital where they had been chosen to get the work done efficiently, while categorically undermining empathic feelings and preventing the establishment of personal attachments and relationships between patients and clinical staff. Times have changed, and so have the organizational systems now prevailing in hospitals. But the example is still instructive, as the problem of how to hold the boundaries and also to handle the strong emotions therapeutically, while nursing often very regressed patients, remains a burning issue.

In my supervision group, the ex-nurses' used defences that were clearly different from the defences used by the non-medically trained counsellors when dealing with their clients' projections constructively. The nurses could draw on their past experiences of being with patients who had regressed because of emotional stress caused by anxieties connected with their debilitating conditions, and they generally demonstrated a calm, professional manner firmly containing their personal affects. While this was useful when dealing with crises states and managing their countertransference reactions, they could at times feel like rather matter-of-fact detached professionals not in touch with the patients' primitive emotional states, and occasionally expecting from them a self-discipline they were not capable of. As their supervisor, I had to help such counsellors modify this stance to a more facilitating empathic attitude, as far as they were capable of letting go such deeply engrained old habits of relating to people in distress, which they had been taught in their previous profession but were no longer appropriate.

Group supervision as a system of using the unconscious dynamics of clinical work

All supervision in the service was done in groups in order to involve the counsellors in supervising each others' work and learning from each other. The analyst and the psychodynamic counsellor in my four-person group proved better equipped to attune to the patients' emotional states and to use their countertransference creatively than the ex-nurses; however, when the clients' somatic states continued to persist they were more liable to flounder, and then confronting their pain could prove immensely difficult for them and unconscious self-destructive attitudes could not be thought about. The group dynamic became fractured when clinical material seemed impossibly recalcitrant, and all this produced powerful competitive tensions, collective moods of commiseration or of impotence, which threatened to sabotage the supervisory containment. Internal conflicts within people became external conflicts between people, and parallel processes blocked the group (Driver, 2002). Only when these were understood as reflections of projective identification on the clients' part could the work be resumed and deepened, but intermittently the supervision could feel severely undermined and almost uncontainable.

At times there was a sense from the counsellors of "it's just too much" and "why me", which clearly picked up on how the clients felt when they complained of the impossibility of their conditions and indicated that they wanted to give up or were overcome by envious, destructive, and hopeless feelings. Then the supervision became a storm-tossed scene, and the challenge was simply to keep one's head above water in order to prevent the ship from being wrecked. In other words, the task was to go on supporting the counsellors and to inspire them to go on hoping and believing in their difficult task of remaining alert and alive to the work.

The necessity of building trust

The counsellors' clients were all contracted for open-ended work, and some of them stayed for years, attached to their counsellors as if they were lifebelts. This depended on having earned and keeping the clients' trust. Some counsellors were better than others at establishing firm working alliances, depending on their management of anxiety levels and on their sheer stamina, and as the supervisor I often had to steer a cautious course in the group, preventing critical clashes between the counsellors or facing joint assaults on myself, when everybody turned against me. There could be fierce resistance to my interventions, and the basic assumptions of pairing or splitting were ever-present threats when disagreement about techniques or diagnostic hypotheses divided the group.

The counsellor who was in charge of assessments had a special place in the group, as she knew more than the others about every client and felt privileged in her position of gate-keeping. As a supervisor, it was important not to question the validity of her judgments, though her psychodynamic perspective occasionally needed some diplomatic sharpening. In some respects she was more exposed and fragile than the others, who were likely to question her prognostic hypotheses, and she tended to feel anxious under the pressure of dual responsibility.

For me as the supervisor the clients were always absent, and my grasp of them was dependent on what the counsellors chose to tell me. I always had to rely on my intuition and on the careful scanning of client profiles for their unconscious dimensions. Inevitably some of the counsellors were more able to persevere and plumb the full depths of their clients' narrative than others, and I was not always able to get to the full truth.

One counsellor in particular was finely attuned to her clients' distress, and this enabled her to help them express their rage and despair in creative ways. There was a toughness in her compassion that communicated itself as containment, and it helped some of her severely damaged clients to climb out of the pit of loneliness and hopelessness they had fallen into, to open up to her, and to risk communication with others. One client in particular learnt to use painting as a containing medium for his chaotic emotions, and others discovered various talents they didn't know they had, which made them feel meaningfully alive. This counsellor was particularly able to use supervision supportively and to enjoy the validation of her efforts as a resource of energy, which spurred her on to further empathic success.

Another counsellor was very intuitive in drawing out her clients' imaginative potential and helped them generate creative ideas constructively. It also meant that they were enabled to turn fantasies into realities and to derive satisfaction and purpose from becoming active in ways that transcended their bleak or passive somatic states. Their lively stories provided dramatic experiences in supervision, though this work could at times also be no more than dabs of bright colour in a landscape of greys and blacks. In fact, the narcissistic aspect to this particular counsellor's casework tended to lead inevitably to many a disappointment, when the serious illness that had brought the client reasserted itself inexorably.

I remember the poignant story of a man who had worked all his life as a bodyguard and had developed a splendid physique that had made him feel omnipotent, until he sprained his ankle and experienced a total deflation of his self-confidence. He became unable to continue in his job, and a tribunal had to be called to assess his fitness for the task. A serious emotional collapse was paralleling the physical breakdown, and this made the therapist's task almost impossibly difficult, since the client had no inner resources whatever to support this unexpected physical impotence and to adjust to his new situation.

Another difficult case was that of a young woman with AIDS who, rather recklessly, had a baby without considering that the baby might be born with AIDS. The counsellor, the client, and the group had a collusive wishful fantasy that the illness might not infect the child, and everybody was devastated when this hope was dashed. It taught us forcefully that working with seriously ill people always requires humility, realism, and keeping one's feet on the ground against the constant temptation of omnipotent wishful thinking in defence against despair.

Maintaining the frame

To go back to the beginning: The guiding principle for the supervisor in this case, as always, was to focus steadily on all the clients' specific complaints and conditions and to maintain the analytic attitude, in particular when the therapeutic couple felt tempted to construct manic defences in denial of pain and distress. Assuming that there is a psychosomatic component to most physical illnesses, the counsellor's work consisted in addressing the psychic component while remaining alert to and aware of the somatic aspects in the constantly shifting scenario. If, in the words of the pianist Glenn Gould, the overall aim was to help the client maintain "the dignity to bear his/her suffering with a hint of quiet resignation", then the counsellor had to be helped to bear in mind constantly that this attitude can conflict with strong emotion and is easily disturbed by unconscious fantasies of recovery, catastrophe, or release that pass between client and counsellor by projective identification. In short, there has to be a constant monitoring in the supervision of seriously ill clients of the subtle mind–body interactions, which at bottom remain unknowable and mysterious while needing to be interpreted in the light of the medical diagnosis and the client's presenting problem. It often turns out that the bipolar field becomes split, and while the supervisor holds the mind, the counsellor focuses on the body of the client, or vice versa.

Fantasies of destruction and infection

Hinshelwood (2004) cautions that "Care is not omnipotent and cannot heal everything. There is a risk of becoming disheartened, burnt out or depressed. As the carers' professional superego constantly encourages them to make high demands on themselves, they can take on unnatural and overwhelming responsibility—that is, become omnipotent or turn a blind eye to reality. Alongside the conscious wish to care there is always the unconscious fantasy about the suffering that needs to be alleviated" (p. 25). Menzies-Lyth (1988) maintained that "the objective situation bears a striking resemblance to the fantasy situation that exists in every individual at the deepest levels of the mind" (p. 440). Hinshelwood (2004) again: "These fantasies are connected with deep concerns about doing violence and damage and they are a powerful motivating force as caring becomes a means for the atonement of violence. Thus there is an unconscious need for the patient which parallels the rejection of them. There is also a fear of infection, and this fear points to fears in the patient" (p. 25). Calling on Winnicott's 1947 paper "Hate in the Countertransference", Hinshelwood points to the passive aggression and to the ambivalence in the carer, which needs reflection rather than action, understanding and not acting out. He also talks of "task drift" as a process that carers are prone to, which makes them move from containment to offering maternal care (p. 116), and he recommends the development of an "internal consultant" to generate reflection and meaning.

Translated into my supervisory task with this particular group of counsellors, this meant ongoing realistic assessment of the counsellors' performance in order to prevent them from becoming disheartened, burnt out, or depressed. "A trouble shared is a trouble halved" could have been the optimistic motto for supervisor and therapist, as it is in many cases, as long as there is some trusting response from the client. Yet the emotional pressures are always relentless, and not everybody stays the course.

REFERENCES

Ashley, J. (1985). A personal account. In: H. Orlans, *Adjustment to Adult Hearing Loss*. London: Taylor & Francis.

Bacon, F. (1668). *The Essays or Counsels, Civil and Moral, of Francis Lord Verulam, Viscount of St Albans*. London: Thomas Ratcliffe & Tho Daniel.

Bettelheim, B. (1980). *Surviving and Other Essays* (pp. 274–314). New York: Vintage Books.

Bion, W. R. (1984). *Learning from Experience*. London: Karnac.

Bion, W. R. (1987). *Second Thoughts*. London: Karnac.

Black, D. M. (2000). The functioning of religions from a modern psychoanalytic perspective. *Mental Health, Religion & Culture, 3* (1): 13–26.

Bowlby, J. (1963). Pathological mourning and childhood mourning. In: R. Frankiel (Ed.), *Essential Papers on Object Loss*. New York: New York University Press.

Camus, A. (1981). *The Stranger*, transl. Stuart Gilbert. New York: Vintage Books/Random House.

Clark, M. (1998). "God could be something terrible." In: I. Alister & C. Hauke (Eds.), *Contemporary Jungian Analysis: Post-Jungian Perspectives from the Society of Analytical Psychology*. London: Routledge.

159

Coltart, N. (1987). Diagnosis and assessment for suitability for psycho-analytical psychotherapy. *British Journal of Psychotherapy, 4* (2): 127–134.

Coren, A. (2001). *Short-Term Psychotherapy—A Psychodynamic Approach.* Hampshire: Palgrave.

Driver, C. (2002). The geography and topography of supervision in a group setting. In: C. Driver & E. Martin (Eds.), *Supervising Psychotherapy.* London: Sage.

Field, N. (Ed.) (2005) (with T. Harvey & B. Sharp). *Ten Lectures on Psychotherapy and Spirituality.* London: Karnac.

Fairbairn, W. R. D. (1944). Endopsychic structures considered in terms of object-relationships. In: *Psychoanalytic Studies of the Personality.* London: Tavistock Publications, 1952.

Fitzerman, B. (1996). Anger—the hidden destroyer—a psychodynamic approach with the physically disabled. *Psychodynamic Counselling* 2 (3).

Fitzgerald, R., & Murray Parkes, C. (1998). Loss of sensory and cognitive functions. In: C. Murray Parkes & A. Markus (Eds.), *Coping with Loss.* London: BMJ Books.

Fonagy, P. (2001). *Attachment Theory and Psychoanalysis.* New York: Other Press.

Frankl, V. E. (1984). *Man's Search for Meaning.* New York: Pocket Books.

Freud, S. (1920). *Beyond the Pleasure Principle. S.E.,* 18.

Freud, S. (1923). *The Ego and the Id. S.E.,* 19.

Freud, S. (1933). *New Introductory Lectures on Psycho-Analysis* [Lecture XXXII: Anxiety and instinctual life]. *S.E.,* 22.

Freud, S. (1940 [1938]). *An Outline of Psycho-Analysis* [Part II, Chap. VI: The technique of psycho-analysis]. *S.E.,* 23.

Gerhardt, S. (2004). *Why Love Matters: How Affection Shapes a Baby's Brain.* Hove/New York: Brunner-Routledge.

Grotstein, J. S. (1993). Foreword. In: N. Symington, *Narcissism: A New Theory.* London Karnac.

Heimann, P. (1952). Certain functions of introjection and projection in early infancy. In: M. Klein, P. Heimann, S. Isaacs, & J. Riviere (Eds.), *Developments in Psychoanalysis.* London: Hogarth Press.

Hinshelwood, R. D. (1991). Psychodynamic formulation in assessment for psychotherapy. *British Journal of Psychotherapy, 8* (2): 166–174.

Hinshelwood, R. D. (2004). *Suffering Insanity*. Hove: Brunner-Routledge.

Joseph, B. (1989). *Psychic Equilibrium and Psychic Change*, ed. M. Feldman & E. B. Spillius. London/New York: Routledge, 1994.

Kaplan-Solms, K., & Solms, M. (2000). *Clinical Studies in Neuro-Psychoanalysis*. London: Karnac.

Kavaler-Adler, S. (2003). *Mourning, Spirituality, and Psychic Change: A New Object Relations View of Psychoanalysis*. Hove: Brunner-Routledge.

Klein, M. (1935). A contribution to the psychogenesis of manic depressive states. *International Journal of Psycho-Analysis*, 16: 145–174.

Klein, M. (1946). Notes on some schizoid mechanism. *International Journal of Psycho-Analysis*, 27: 99–110.

Klein, M (1955). On identification. In: *New Directions in Psycho-Analysis*, ed. M. Klein, P. Heimann, & R. Money-Kyrle. London: Tavistock Publications.

Klein, M (1957). *Envy and Gratitude and Other Works 1946–1963*. London: Tavistock Publications.

Kohut, H. (1968).The psychoanalytic treatment of narcissistic personality disorders: Outline of a systematic approach. In: A. Esman (Ed.), *Essential Papers on Transference*. New York: New York University Press, 1990.

Kohut, H. (1971). *The Analysis of the Self: A Systemic Approach to the Treatment of Narcissistic Personality Disorders*. New York: International Universities Press.

Kohut, H. (1977). *The Restoration of the Self*. New York: International Universities Press.

Kohut, H. (1980). *Advances in Self Psychology*. New York: International Universities Press.

Lendrum, S., & Syme, G. (2004). *Gift of Tears: A Practical Approach to Loss and Bereavement in Counselling and Psychotherapy* (2nd edition). Hove: Brunner-Routledge.

Main, T. F. (1957). The ailment. *British Journal of Medical Psychology*, 30 (Part 3): 129–145.

Malan, D. H. (1979). *Individual Psychotherapy and the Science of Psychodynamics*. Oxford: Butterworth-Heinemann, 1994.

McDougall, J. (1989). *Theatres of the Body*. London: Free Association Books.

Menzies-Lyth, I. (1988). The functioning of social systems as a defence against anxiety. In: *Containing Anxiety in Institutions: Selected Essays*. London: Free Association Books.

Mitrani, J. L. (2001). "Taking the transference": Notes on some technical implications in three papers by Bion. *International Journal of Psychoanalysis, 82*: 1085–1104.

Murray Parkes, C. (1972). *Bereavement: Studies of Grief in Adult Life*. London: Tavistock Publications.

Nouwen, H. J. M. (1990). *Reaching Out*. London: Fount Paperbacks.

O'Donnell, K. (2003). *Postmodernism*. Oxford: Lion Publishing.

Ogden, T. H. (1989). The initial analytic meeting. In: *The Primitive Edge of Experience*. London: Karnac.

O'Gorman, M. P. (2000) "The kick-off head crew": Psychotherapeutic work with acquired brain-injury on an NHS neurological rehabilitation unit. *Psychoanalytic Psychotherapy, 15* (1): 61–79.

Parkinson, J. (2003). Intruder in the night: Cancer and the "I" within. *Journal of Psychotherapy, 19* (4): 415–433. [Special Issue: *On the Body*.]

Peters, R. (1991). The therapist's expectation of the transference. *Journal of Analytical Psychology, 36*: 77–92.

Pincus, L. (1974). *Death and the Family: The Importance of Mourning*. New York: Pantheon.

Rosenfeld, H. (1987). *Impasse and Interpretation*. London: Tavistock Publications.

Samuels, A. (2001). *Politics on the Couch: Citizenship and the Internal Life*. London: Profile Books.

Samuels, A., Shorter, B., & Plaut, F. (1986). *A Critical Dictionary of Jungian Analysis*. London: Routledge & Kegan Paul.

Sandler, J., Dare, C., & Holder, A. (1973). *The Patient and the Analyst*. London: Karnac, 1993.

Sontag, S. (1983). *Illness as Metaphor*. London: Penguin.

Speck, P. (1994). Working with dying people: On being good enough. In: A. Obholzer & V. Zagier Roberts (Eds.), *The Unconscious at Work*. London: Routledge.

Symington, N. (1986). The analyst's act of freedom as agent of therapeutic change. In: G. Kohon (Ed.), *The British School of Psychoanalysis: The Independent Tradition*. London: Free Association Books.

Symington, N. (1993). *Narcissism: A New Theory*. London: Karnac.

Tillich, P. (1952). *The Courage to Be*. London: Fontana.

Wallace, P. (1989). "Emotional Adaptation in Serious Illness—Therapist and Client Perspectives." Unpublished MSc dissertation, University of Surrey.

Williams, M. (2004). *The Velveteen Rabbit*. London: Egmont Books.

Winnicott, D. W. (1947). Hate in the countertransference. In: *Through Paediatrics to Psychoanalysis*. London: Hogarth Press & The Institute of Psychoanalysis, 1975.

Winnicott, D. W. (1949). Mind and its relation to the psyche-soma. In: *Through Paediatrics to Psychoanalysis* (pp. 243–254). London: Hogarth Press and The Institute of Psycho-Analysis, 1975.

Winnicott, D. W. (1954). Inter-relationship of body disease and psychological disorder. In: *Human Nature*. London: Free Association Books, 1988.

Winnicott, D. W. (1956). *Through Paediatrics to Psychoanalysis*. London: Hogarth Press and The Institute of Psycho-Analysis, 1975.

Winnicott, D. W. (1960). Ego distortion in terms of true and false self. In: *The Maturational Processes and the Facilitating Environment*. London: Karnac, 1990.

Winnicott, D. W. (1971). *Playing and Reality*. London: Tavistock Publications.

INDEX

abandonment, sense of, 34, 36, 55, 88
  in face of life-threatening illness,
    31
abuse, sexual, 42, 44
acceptance, 24, 26, 90, 116, 120
  good-enough, 21, 27
  struggle for, in face of serious
    illness, 24–28
acoustic neuroma, 30
acupuncture, 118
aggression, 57–59, 87, 157
AIDS, 4–5, 51, 123, 129–131, 141, 156
ambivalence, 58, 87, 90, 157
anger, 26, 75, 78, 81, 86, 89–90, 127, 134,
    140
  clinical vignettes:
    Anne, 116–117, 119–120
    Chay, 52–56, 60–61
    Marc, 44–45, 48–49
    Valerie, 96–97, 99, 101, 103
  at diagnosis of serious illness, 20
  lack of focus for, 24
  maternal, 53
  repression of, 23
Anne: cerebral palsy (clinical
    vignette), 104–122

anxiety(ies), 19–20, 26, 37, 77, 88, 93,
    116–117, 134, 138, 150–154
  clinical vignette: Marc/Mr M, 45,
    47–48, 57
  in face of serious illness, 22
  ontological, 126
  paranoid, 57
  of threat of non-being, 126
  transferential, 135
  unconscious, 16, 151
archaic grandiose self, 52, 54
Archer, R., xi, xv–xvi, 1–6, 112–122,
    136–148
arthritis, 82
Ashley, J., 93
assessment, 3, 5, 13, 10–13, 40, 60, 88,
    97, 154, 157
  interview, 9–12, 17, 65, 113
  process, 80–81
Association for Pastoral and Spiritual
    Care and Counselling, 132
attachment, 52, 62
  primary, 42, 101
auxiliary ego, therapist as, 152
awe, feelings of, in face of serious
    illness, 26

Bacon, F., 63–64
BACUP, 2
Balint, M., 87
basic assumptions of pairing or splitting, 154
bereavement, 70, 93, 111, 140, 143, 147
Berger, S., xi, 40–50
Beth: living with a life-threatening tumour (clinical vignette), 29–39
Bettelheim, B., 64
Bion, W. R., 57, 89–90
Black, D. M.., xv–xx, 132
blindness, 16, 81, 121, 157
blood disorder(s), 4, 12
Blows, D., xv, 2
body-image, 85
body–mind integration, 8
boundary, issues of, 140–143
Bowlby, J., 96
Breathing Space, 4
British Association for Counselling and Psychotherapy, 132

Camus, A., 63–64
cancer, 2, 4, 110, 121–123, 151
    breast, 25, 133–134
    cervical, 85
    lung, 143
Cancerlink, 2
cerebral palsy, 4, 83
    clinical vignette: Anne, 104–122
Chant, L., xi–xii, 63–78
Chay: living with HIV/AIDS (clinical vignette), 51–62
"cheeky" behaviour as defence (clinical vignette), 96–101
chemotherapy, 23, 25
Clark, M., 132
clients, home or hospital visits to, 4, 138, 140–143
Cobb, F., 2
cognitive functions, impaired, result of, 92
Coltart, N., 10, 11
communication, meaningful, in therapy (clinical vignette: Valerie), 92–103
compensation, financial claim for, 81
confidentiality, 147
constipation, 151

container/containment, 16, 31, 55–56, 58, 90, 97, 99, 152, 154–155, 157
    /contained, 89
    counsellor as, 86
    therapeutic, 96
"continuity of being", 8–9, 13, 15
control, feeling of loss of, in face of serious illness, 25
Coren, A., 100
countertransference, 15, 52, 54, 59, 78, 91, 112, 120, 150–153
    and transference, 86–90
creativity, 57–59, 62, 151
    search for (clinical vignette: Beth), 29–39
cystic fibrosis, 4
Cystic Fibrosis Trust, 4

Dare, C., 89, 90
"dark night of the soul", 128
deaf client, counselling (clinical vignette: Valerie), 92–103
deafness, 112
death, 6, 21, 28, 50, 78, 83, 88, 93, 101, 111, 121, 126, 127, 149
    counselling and psychotherapy, 136–148
    fear of, 135, 138
    instinct, 58, 87
    as letting go, 146
    living with (clinical vignettes):
        Beth, 29–39
        Chay, 51–62
        Marc/Mr M, 47, 49
        Mark, 128–135
    -wish, unconscious, 27
defence(s), 81, 100, 150
    control as, 57
    denial as, 138
    destructive, 82
    against expressing anger, 24
    healthy, 82, 87, 91, 115, 117
    manic, 82, 156
    omnipotent, 52, 54, 61, 117, 156
    projective identification as, 57
    splitting as, 89
    in supervision, 152–153
degenerative conditions, 83
denial, 15, 33, 138, 156
    at diagnosis of serious illness, 21
    primitive state of, 151

see also disbelief
dependency, issues of, 11, 16, 47, 81, 85, 88, 115–116
depletion, feelings of, in face of serious illness, 25
depression, 13–14, 26–27, 57, 61, 70, 78, 150
    clinical vignette: Marc/Mr M, 40, 42, 49
    in face of serious illness, 23
depressive position, 52
despair, 20, 61, 66, 70, 89, 120, 134, 155, 156
    at diagnosis of serious illness, 21
destruction, fantasies of, 157–158
diabetes, 21
    clinical vignette: Marc/Mr M, 14–17, 40–50
diagnosis of serious illness:
    effects of, 18–28
    initial/early reactions to, 19–22
dialysis, 45–46, 48
disability, social stigma of, 84
disbelief, 21
    at diagnosis of serious illness, 21
    see also denial
distaste, feelings of, in face of serious illness, 26
Dixon-Nuttall, R., xii, 4, 63–78
drawing, *see* painting/drawing
dread, feelings of, 27
    in face of serious illness, 26
dream(s), 20–21
    clinical examples:
        Beth, 37
        Chay, 59, 61
        Lavinia, 78
        Mark, 129–130
Driver, C., 154

ego:
    development, 60
    splitting of, 58
    strength, 13, 61, 80
entrapment, feelings of, 32, 37
envy, 54–55, 57, 88, 144
epilepsy, 4, 84
    temporal-lobe, 76
Evans, G., xii, 7–17

Fairbairn, W. R. D., 87, 90–91

father, absent, 53
fear, 21–23, 26, 66, 70, 75, 76, 93, 116, 117, 127, 128, 131, 145
    of being overwhelmed, 39
    of chaos, 54
    of death, 135, 138
    of dialysis (clinical vignette: Marc/Mr M), 46–47
    of fragmentation, 81
    of infection, 157
    of loss of control over one's body, 84
    of unknown, 23, 138, 144
Field, N., 132
Fitzgerald, R., 92–93
Fonagy, P., 8
frame, maintenance of, 156–157
    see also boundary
Frankl, V. E., 127
Freud, S., 85, 87, 90–91
friendship, 63

gastrostomy, 104, 118–119
Gerhardt, S., 8
Gould, G., 156
Green, A., xii–xiii, 104–111
grief, 30–31, 121
    counselling, 78
    at diagnosis of serious illness, 21
    stages of, 28
Grotstein, J. S., 87
group supervision, 153–154

Hatfield, L., xiii, xvii, 79–91
Heap, M., 2
hearing impairments, 4
heart disease, 123
Heimann, P., 60
helplessness, 30, 89, 115, 120, 135, 140, 144
Heythrop College, 117
Hinshelwood, R. D., 12, 157
HIV/AIDS, 83, 151
    living with (clinical vignettes):
        Chay, 51–62
        Mark, 128–135
Holder, A., 89–90
home visits to clients, 3–4, 22, 50, 83, 138, 140–143
hopelessness, 29, 54, 59, 66, 89, 150, 155
horror, feelings of, 27
    in face of serious illness, 26

hospital visits to clients, 3–4, 22, 50, 83, 138, 140–143
hydrocephalus, 110, 113
hypochondriacal states, 9
hysterectomy, 25, 116

IBS, 151
identity, loss of, 33
illness (*passim*):
    serious, predominant emotions associated with, 22–24
individuation, 125
    –separation, 52, 54
infantile object relationships, 12
infection, fear of, 157–158
internal object(s), 37, 90
    persecutory, 95
    relationship, 12
interpretation(s), 10, 16, 98, 135
    appropriateness and timing of, 86
intrapsychic conflict(s), 79
introjection, 95
isolation, sense of, 31, 47, 53, 84, 119, 145
    in face of serious illness, 24

John of The Cross, St, 128
Joseph, B., 16, 110, 113, 121
Jung, C. G., 99, 125

Kaplan-Solms, K., 81
Kavaler-Adler, S., 96
Kelly, M., xiii, 92–103
keloid scars, 26
kidney failure, 40, 46, 48
Klein, M., 52, 55, 57–58
Kohut, H., 53, 59, 86–87, 89, 91

Lavinia: schizophrenia—therapeutic journey (clinical vignette), 63–78
learning difficulties, 4, 113
Lendrum, S., 97
life:
    instinct, 87
    stories, constructing, 150
linking, attacks on, 57
loneliness, 16, 155
    sense of, in face of serious illness, 24
loss of personal identity, 25

Main, T. F., 139
Malan, D. H., 10
Mander, G., xiii, xvi, 149–158
Marc/Mr M: client with uncontrolled diabetes (clinical vignette), 13–17, 40–50
Mark: living with HIV/AIDS (clinical vignette), 128–135
masochism, 87
mastectomy, 25–26
McDougall, J., 79
ME, 4–5, 151
meaning, search for, 1, 127
    clinical vignette: Beth, 29–39
medication, anti-psychotic, 75
meningioma (clinical vignette: Beth), 30–39
meningitis, 110, 121
Menninger, K., 65
Menzies-Lyth, I., 152, 157
mirroring, 54–55, 86
Mitrani, J. L., 86, 90
mother–infant relationship, 8, 91
mothering, good-enough, 86
multiple sclerosis, 4, 19, 21, 151
Murray Parkes, C., 28, 92–93

narcissistic wound, 53, 58
narratives, constructing, 150
Neary, A., 2
negative therapeutic reaction, 58
neurological symptoms/illness, 20
neuropathy, 14, 49
Nightall, C., xiv, xvi, 18–28
Nouwen, H. J. M., 132

object relations, 12, 133
O'Donnell, K., 124
oedipal issues, 32
Ogden, T. H., 10, 11
O'Gorman, M. P., 80–81, 86
omnipotence, 52, 61, 89
omnipotent defence, 54, 117
omnipotent phantasies of cure, 139
omnipotent wishful thinking as defence, 156
ontological insecurity, 87, 91
orchidectomy, 26
organ transplant, 4, 14, 17, 40, 43, 46, 48, 50, 151

pain, 11, 20, 23, 46, 49, 54, 92, 133, 144, 153, 156
  clinical vignettes:
    Anne, 109–111, 113, 115–116, 118, 121
    Beth, 30–31
    Lavinia, 73, 75, 77
    Valerie, 96–103
  "point of maximum", 12–13, 16
painting/drawing, 75, 78, 101, 155
  use of in therapy, 151
    clinical vignettes: Beth, 31–39
    Chay, 58 Lavinia, 74
paranoid–schizoid position, 52, 57
paraplegia, 4
parental conflict, 15
Parkinson, J., xiv, xvi, 123–135
persecutory world view, 102
personal identity, loss of, in face of serious illness, 25
Peters, R., 56
Pincus, L., 28
Plaut, F., 125
projection(s), 24, 38, 45, 54, 115, 140, 144, 150, 151, 153
  clinical vignette: Valerie, 95, 100
  as defence, 82
  of unbearable feelings, 89
projective identification, 57, 154, 156
psyche:
  definition, 8
  and soma, 8, 79
psychodynamic therapy (passim)
psychosomatic illness, 9

radiotherapy, 23, 25, 30
rage, 11, 16, 31, 37, 53, 58–59, 89, 96, 155
  murderous, 34
recrimination, thoughts of, 23
  in face of serious illness, 22
referral, 10
regression, 25, 27, 32, 97, 153
  defensive, 151
renal damage, 14
repetition compulsion, 16
resentment, 12, 83, 86
  in face of serious illness, 22
resistance, 59, 81–82, 91, 115, 139, 154
retinopathy, 14, 40
Rosenfeld, H., 57

Royal Marsden Hospital, 31
Russell, G., 2

sadism, 87
sadness, 38, 61, 66, 78, 98, 100–101, 121
  at diagnosis of serious illness, 21
Samuels, A., 125
Sandler, J., 89–90
schizophrenia, 70, 74
  therapeutic journey (clinical vignette: Lavinia), 63–78
self-pity at diagnosis of serious illness, 22
sensory functions, impaired, result of, 92
separation and attachment, 36
Serious Physical Illness Counselling Service, 2
sexual abuse, 42, 44
Shorter, B., 125
sign language, 94
skin rash and anger (clinical vignette: Chay), 52–53, 55–56, 61
Snowdon, L., xiv, 51–62
Solms, M., 81
"somatizers", 151
Sontag, S., 7
Speck, P., 135
speech/hearing problems, 112
spiritual dimension in therapy, 123–135
spirituality, definition of, 124–125
splitting, 58, 82, 89, 151, 154
Steffens, D., xiv, 29–39
stigma:
  of deafness, 94
  social, of disability, 84
stroke, 12, 30, 123
suicidal feelings in face of serious illness, 26
suicidal ideation/thoughts/feelings, 5, 14, 23, 26, 89, 120
suicide, 89, 120, 133
superego, professional, carers', 157
supervision, 3, 5, 78, 135, 138, 147
  group, 62, 74, 77, 80, 134, 153–154
  of work with seriously ill patients, 149–158
surgery, 23, 25–26, 30, 77, 118, 143

symbiosis, 54
Syme, G., 97
Symington, N., 59–60, 87, 91

talking cure, therapy as, 92
termination, of therapy, 100–102
therapeutic alliance, 11, 52, 54, 56, 137,
     142, 151
therapeutic setting, 83
therapist (*passim*):
   attendance of at funeral, 147
   as auxiliary ego, 152
   as container, 96
   idealization of, 89
   role of with terminally ill patient,
      137–140
therapy (*passim*):
   spiritual dimension in, 123–135
   as "talking cure", 92
   termination of, 100–102
Tillich, P., 126
transference, 13, 16, 97, 101, 114, 120,
     145
   and countertransference, 86–90
   idealizing, 89
   interpretations, 86, 90, 139
   negative, 52, 88, 90, 96, 103
      development of, 56–60
   positive, 96, 103
   relationship, 12, 87, 90
   resolution of, 138
   "taking", 86

transplants, organ, 4, 14, 17, 40, 43, 46,
     48, 50, 151
trust, 39, 62, 69, 75–76, 78, 85, 138
   need to build, 154–156
tumour, life-threatening, living with
      (clinical vignette: Beth), 29–39

ulcers, 151

Valerie: counselling deaf client
      (clinical vignette), 92–103
viral encephalitis, 84
visual and hearing impairments, 4

Wallace, P., 5, 120
Westminster Pastoral Foundation, 1,
     64, 74, 105, 130
William Kyle Centre, 3, 64, 121
Williams, M., 127
Winnicott, D. W., 8, 62, 79, 86–87, 91,
     126, 157
withdrawal in face of serious illness,
     24
WPF Counselling and Psychotherapy,
     1–3, 13, 64–66, 69–70, 74,
     76–77, 106, 112–113, 115,
     121–122, 141
   assessment interview, 9–11, 80–81
   supervision of counsellors, 80,
      149–158
WPF Serious Physical Illness Service,
      xv–xvii, 2, 74